Luton Town FC in the 1970s

Cover design and photograph by Paul Rance

ISBN: 9798387421211
Imprint: Independently published

A booksmusicfilmstv.com book

Contents

Introduction (originally published in April 2017 with the paperback and Kindle editions)

Luton Town FC in the 1970s was, for the most part, like any other decade for a Town supporter - great highs, great lows, financial difficulties, and waiting for the inevitable sale of the club's best players.

There were, however, two things that made the 1970s slightly different. Firstly, with Eric Morecambe as a Luton Town director, the Hatters could expect a mention on *The Morecambe & Wise Show* every Christmas! Bearing in mind that half the country's population would be tuning in, any mention was welcome publicity and made Luton seem like a cool club to support. Secondly, in Harry Haslam and David Pleat, Luton appointed two managers who knew how to spot and nurture young talent (Haslam even tried to sign a 17-year-old Diego Maradona, when manager of Sheffield United). While, under Pleat, the likes of Ricky Hill, Brian Stein and Mal Donaghy blossomed, and they would become the base of Luton's greatest side in the 1980s. Consequently, when appointed in 1978, David Pleat became the most significant managerial appointment in Luton's history.

A best of Luton XI from the 1970s would probably have won the League, too! But Malcolm MacDonald, Don Givens and Paul Futcher were never likely to have career-long stays at Kenilworth Road. But, here is a tasty XI made up of players who played for the Town in the '70s: Jake Findlay;

Kirk Stephens, Mal Donaghy, Chris Nicholl, Paul Futcher; Ricky Hill, Andy King, Peter Anderson; Malcolm MacDonald, Brian Stein, Don Givens.

In this book, you'll find my personal recollections of the 1970s from a fan who watched in awe games at Kenilworth Road as a 10-year-old, but had become cynical at promotion near misses by the end of the decade. Luckily, I also wasn't really a victim of the rampant hooliganism of the 1970s, apart from getting clobbered with a bicycle chain when a teenager, by another teenager, in a random act of violence when coming out of a testimonial game!

Anyway, if you want to support a team where everything is nice and safe then don't support Luton! Enjoy.

- Paul Rance, April 2017.

1969-70 - Nice Beginnings...

1970 couldn't have started off much worse than it did. A 5-1 defeat at Shrewsbury on January 10th was followed by a 2-0 reverse against Plymouth Argyle at Kenilworth Road a week later. But Town fans shouldn't have worried, as Malcolm MacDonald helped Luton to the runners-up spot in Division Three behind Orient. Supermac scored 13 times in the second half of the 1969-70 season, which included a hat-trick in a 5-0 home thumping of Reading. Luton were also the best supported club in the division, averaging 14,808 per home game. MacDonald ended up with 28 goals in his first season for the Hatters. Not bad for a converted full-back! It's funny, that as with another Luton goalscoring legend, Joe Payne, Luton had found themselves a top striker, after converting him from another position.

Luton's promotion was sealed at Mansfield (often a graveyard for Luton sides through the years) with a 0-0 draw on April 20th.

Luton's regular line-up in 1969-70 was: Sandy Davie; John Ryan, Jack Bannister, Chris Nicholl, Alan Slough; John Collins, Mike Keen, Graham French; Malcolm MacDonald, Matt Tees, Keith Allen.

1970-71 - The Rise and Rise of Supermac

I began following the Hatters in the 1970-71 season, and the first match I attended was a pre-season friendly against Burnley from the First Division. Luton lost 2-1. I stood in the Oak Road End, and, strangely, my most abiding memory was of Burnley 'keeper Tony Waiters kicking the ball so far I thought it'd end up on the Moon.

Watching football live for the first time also showed everything writ large, and TV has never really got close to matching the feel of watching a game in the flesh. While the four-year-old Hatters fan nearby seemed to rub in the fact that I had waited till I was ten before going to my first game. It should have happened when I was nine - I had planned going to my first Luton match at the beginning of the 1969-70 season, but it didn't happen because I suspect the friend I planned going with was a closet Hornets fan.

In '70-'71 Luton had a good side, and, as is so often the case with Luton's best players, several of them became big names after moving from Kenilworth Road. The most notable Hatters star of the 1970s was Luton number 9 Malcolm MacDonald, aka Supermac as he was christened by the Oak Road End. In those days the Kenilworth Road End was reserved for the away supporters and Hatters fans who didn't mind risking a drenching on the open terrace.

It was Luton fringe player Rodney Green's son and my maternal Grandfather who really got me into football. Rodney's son lived opposite my bungalow in Laburnum Grove in the Warden Hill area of Luton. While Rodney's claim to fame was that he was the first player to score a hat-trick against Ray Clemence in Clem's professional career. More on Ray Clemence's banter with a Luton fan, and on the second player to score a hat-trick against Ray later.

Luton's first game back in the Second Division was a 4-2 defeat at Bolton. This was also Town stalwart Terry Branston's last game for the Hatters, and a Terry Wharton hat-trick for the Trotters made it an opener as impressive as a Del Boy bargain...

The next League game was my first. It was a 0-0 draw against Norwich at Kenilworth Road in August, 1970. That was not an accurate indicator of what following Luton Town was going to be like. Dull it would rarely be. Jimmy Ryan made his full League debut for the Town in that game. Luton were impressive in the early stages of the season, and notable results included 4-0 home wins against Oxford and Orient. Luton also drew at Birmingham, won narrowly at QPR, and beat Middlesbrough at home. A narrow 1-0 defeat at eventual champions Leicester was Luton's only other setback going into October.

A 3-0 win at Kenilworth Road against Bristol City meant that, when the mighty Arsenal came to the Hatters home patch for a League Cup tie, Luton had yet to concede a goal in their first 6 home League and cup games of the season. A huge crowd of 27,023 turned up, and I was one of them. It was the biggest crowd at Kenilworth Road since the late 1950s, and a plucky 1-0 defeat wasn't too difficult to bear. More so, if I'd known that Arsenal would win the Double that season. Arsenal were also my second team. It seemed as if all the football mad kids in Luton then had either a second team, or didn't support Luton at all, but the Manchester Uniteds and Leeds Uniteds of this world.

Luton hardly had a hangover though from the Arsenal game. Five days later a kickabout with friends in Laburnum Close came to an abrupt end as we rushed home to watch *The Big Match*. The nation was about to see the birth of a superstar, and it was Malcolm MacDonald. Supermac had hit a hat-trick in a 5-1 demolition of Sheffield Wednesday at Hillsborough the previous day. The Owls had also been a First Division side only a few months earlier, and it was, in truth, a staggering scoreline. Two successive 2-0 home wins, against Bolton Wanderers and Blackburn Rovers respectively, further emphasised that the Hatters were serious promotion contenders.

With no goals conceded at home in the League until

a 2-1 loss to Sunderland in late October, and impressive away form, Luton had players who were to become big names in English football in the '70s.

Malcolm MacDonald was certainly not the only star in the team. Centre-half Chris Nicholl was also a highly promising young player, and Don Givens was MacDonald's strike partner. MacDonald became British football's most expensive striker when he moved to Newcastle United in May, 1971 for £180,000, and World Cup winner Martin Peters, then Britain's most expensive player (when joining Spurs from West Ham around a year earlier) had gone for only £20,000 more.

Don Givens would go on to become a key part of a QPR side that narrowly missed winning the League title in 1976. He also went on to become Eire's leading goalscorer, while Supermac achieved two noteworthy feats when capped at full level by England. He scored one of the goals that helped defeat world champions West Germany 2-0 at Wembley in 1975, and he scored all 5 goals in a 5-0 thumping of Cyprus, again at Wembley in the same year. The old stadium wasn't to be so kind to Malcolm re cup finals, though, as he was on the losing side in all three finals he played there - two for Newcastle and one for Arsenal.

MacDonald and Givens would have graced any top flight side in the '70s - even a title-winning one. But Luton always needed the revenue generated by transfers. While, good though Givens was, I think his miss in one game was the worst I've ever seen from a Luton player. In front of an unguarded net he somehow managed to smack the ball over the crossbar - shades of Ronny Rosenthal.

Englishman Nicholl would go on to captain Aston Villa to League Cup glory in 1977, and he also became an international - with Northern Ireland. Other players of the '70-'71 side included John Ryan, who exceeded expectations when he had a successful career in the top flight at Norwich City years later as a midfielder, fans favourite, winger Jimmy Ryan, and Alan Slough, who played in the 1975 FA Cup final for Fulham alongside the likes of Bobby Moore and Alan Mullery. Slough was a stalwart of Luton's Division Four days, as was the eccentric John Moore, Nicholl's partner in the centre of defence. Midfielder Mike Keen, who had had a great career under Town manager Alec Stock at QPR, captained the 1970-71 side.

Some of Luton's other midfielders are players who have somewhat faded from the memory such as Roger Hoy - "Roger! Roger! Roger! Hoy! Hoy! Hoy!" the Oak Road sang. Another was record £35,000 signing from Arsenal before the 1970-71 season, David Court.

A promising forward at the club was Viv Busby, who later joined Supermac at Newcastle, and they both played in the infamous FA Cup defeat to Hereford in 1971-72. The next season the Magpies suffered another shocking exit, as two John Aston goals at St. James' Park clinched a 2-0 4th Round win for the Hatters. More on that game later.

Luton remained unbeaten in November and December, and highlights included a 2-0 win at high-fliers Hull City, a 2-1 win at home to Sheffield

United, who were eventually promoted, and a 1-0 win at Watford. I had, at the time, yet to fully comprehend the Luton-Watford thing, so it was just like another away win. While a 3-3 draw with Carlisle United was probably the most entertaining League game at Kenilworth Road all season.

With hardly a foreign player to be seen in English football in the early 1970s, even Division Two had, in the 1970-71 season, players who would have walked into the current England side - namely the likes of Leicester City's Peter Shilton, Sunderland's Colin Todd, QPR's Rodney Marsh, and Sheffield United's Tony Currie.

Tony Currie was to entertain us in early December, and almost 20,000 turned up for the Sheffield United game. I watched from the Oak Road End as Currie scored a penalty in front of us, and then blew a kiss to the jeering Luton faithful. Respect. Tony was a former Watford player, so he probably knew what was coming as he strode up to take the spot kick! Currie was a fantastic player, and he became a regular in the England side when with the Blades. That was another aspect of early 1970s football. It seemed that then England managers didn't just consider players from glamorous clubs. The same was true in the 1980s too, with Ricky Hill, Brian Stein, Paul Walsh and Mick Harford all winning England caps when they were at Luton.

Luton's FA Cup adventure was short and sweet in 1970-71. A 1-1 draw at Nottingham Forest rekindled memories of the 1959 FA Cup final, and, in my childish mind, I saw the replay at Kenilworth Road as some kind of chance of revenge. Strangely, the replay was on a Monday, and two days after a 0-0 home draw with QPR. Over 22,000 turned up for that one, and over 23,000 for the Forest game. So, over 45,000 through the Kenny turnstiles in two days - a record of sorts I suspect.

Luton lost a classic cup tie to Forest 4-3, but worse than the result against the First Division side was the hat-trick Malcolm MacDonald scored. If Hatters fans were worried we were going to lose our star player before the Forest game, then his four goals (he also scored at the City Ground) against top flight opposition made it certain that top clubs were going to come up with serious money for him very soon.

Supermac was a bandy-legged powerhouse of a striker, with electric pace, and one iconic photograph of him is from the game at the City Ground. A goalpost had collapsed with Malcolm nearby. The kids of today may not believe it, but Malcolm MacDonald demolished goalposts as well as defences, and he ate five Shredded Wheat...

My paternal Grandmother had died during a grim December and January, which had seen Luton play only five League games because of bad weather. I remember a copper telling me, as I was on my way to a game that it had been postponed. I thought he may have been joking, but you should always trust a policeman, right? He saved me a six mile round trip anyway. I was that fanatical that I was walking in the snow, and to hell with whether buses were running. I was now 11, and my fanaticism was getting out of hand!

I had a black and white scarf and bobble hat then. I also had a Luton Town kit, with a black number 9 on the back of my shirt, which also had the club badge on. The only non-playing adult around that time who wore a football shirt with a number on was Brian Glover, when thinking he was Bobby Charlton in the film *Kes*.

Shanks and Turner was the place to go in Luton for your footie kits. Wally Shanks and Gordon Turner were nice guys, and they gave me some free tracksuit bottoms because they could see that I was, er, enthusiastic. I also had a vague notion that Wally and Gordon might have played for the Town...

Successive narrow away defeats at Blackburn and Sheffield United (in front of a whopping crowd of 30,986) hit Luton's promotion chances, particularly the defeat at promotion rivals United. Interspersed between these two defeats, the Town had played a friendly at home to Coventry in late January. They'd also hosted an Australian XI in November. In the Aussie team was future Hatters favourite Adrian Alston - the Aussies won 2-1.

A 1-0 home win against Watford put Luton back on track in mid-February. Though there was some disappointment that the crowd was only 20,139. A 1-0 win at Portsmouth, and a goalless draw against Sunderland at Roker Park then underlined the solidity of the Town's defence. The defence was as much a strength of the '70-'71 team, as was its attacking threat.

March was to prove to be a disappointing month, with home draws against Charlton and Millwall, but a 3-1 win over Hull at Kenilworth Road was a highlight. Both away games were long treks up north and ended in defeat - 1-0 at Carlisle, and 2-1 at Middlesbrough. Narrow defeats were becoming too much of a recurring theme for Luton as we were entering the business end of the season. First up in April was Birmingham City and it was a blockbuster.

Birmingham and Luton were right in the promotion mix, and 10,000 Brummies travelled down to swell the crowd to one of over 25,000 - the Town's biggest League crowd of the season.

This game was also fascinating because of two young strikers creating a buzz around the country - Luton's 21-year-old striker Malcolm MacDonald and Birmingham's 16-year-old starlet, Trevor Francis. Francis had scored 16 goals in his first 16 League games, including four in one match against Bolton. No teenage forward had made such an impact on English football since Jimmy Greaves in the 1950s. Chants of "Supermac!" from Luton fans were met with cries of "Superboy!" from City fans.

An eye-opener for me, as I queued to get in the Oak Road End, was Birmingham women! One female teenage City fan I remember was taking no crap from the police, shouting "Bollocks!" at one bemused cop. The Oak Road End was segregated, though I seemed to be surrounded by Birmingham fans. But all was well, as a Brum couple held me up to help me get a better view over the zillions of heads.

Luton went 2-0 down (with Bob Latchford scoring

one of the goals. Both he and Francis were in the England team by the end of the decade), and it looked like the promotion dream was coming to an end. But, in a game suitable for the occasion, the Town came storming back to win 3-2, thanks to a cracker from Alan Slough.

The joy of that victory was short-lived, however, as Luton's normally reliable defence fell apart over Easter, and a 3-2 defeat at Bristol City and a 4-0 hammering at Millwall consigned the Town to another season in Division Two.

Missing out on promotion was then rubbed in, as Leicester City's promotion party was next in Town, with another invasion of 10,000 fans (Leicester have never been that small little club the media would have had you believe in the 2015-16 season). A young Peter Shilton was in goal for the Foxes, and Rodney Fern impressed me more than any other opposing player that season I remember. Luton crashed to a 3-1 defeat, and Leicester ended the season as deserved Second Division champions.

A 2-2 home draw against Sheffield Wednesday was witnessed by a crowd of only 12,308, and my one memory was of poor Wednesday star Johnny Sissons copping it from a team-mate for a poor corner, "Ah, Johnny, you c**t!". I know who the potty mouth was, but I won't say, as he was a tough little Scot...

The season ended in anti-climax, but Supermac gave us a parting gift with a hat-trick in the last game of the season - a 3-0 home win over Cardiff City (which also earnt us qualification into the pre-season Watney Cup). The Town finished 6th, which, at the beginning of the season, would have been seen as pretty good by most Hatters fans. But, the fact that the Town fell away near the end of the season left me disappointed. We also kinda knew that no promotion probably meant no Supermac, and so it proved...

Newcastle's bid of £180,000 for Malcolm MacDonald in May was hardly likely to be rejected by cash strapped Luton. Indeed, it wasn't.

My Mother broke the news of Supermac's departure, in four words, after I arrived home from Warden Hill Junior School: "They've sold Malcolm MacDonald." No! Supermac leaving caused me to go into a blub overload. But my cousin reacted the same when Bruce Rioch was sold. Supporting Luton has always involved being prepared for the worst, because it normally happens!

My Mother was the kindest woman I ever knew. But, she did seem to take a sadistic glee in telling people years later how I stood in my school cap on our doorstep crying my eyes out, because Malcolm MacDonald had been sold to Newcastle. Supermac had a spectacular debut for the Toon Army, too, and he scored a hat-trick at St. James' Park against Liverpool and Ray Clemence. Thus, after Rodney Green, MacDonald was the second player to score a treble against Ray Clemence.

My late Father met Malcolm MacDonald at an event once, and said that Malcolm was a nice fella. Dad wasn't a football fan, so meeting Supermac didn't mean so much to him. That's always the way...

1971-72 - Post-Supermac Blues

Manchester United legends George Best, Bobby
Charlton and Denis Law softened the bitter pill of
Malcolm MacDonald's departure to some degree,
when they arrived at Kenilworth Road for a pre-
season friendly. Was George Best really THAT
good? Absolutely. In pretty much all cases if you
are expecting something amazing you're left
disappointed. Not with George. I did also see him
play for Dunstable Town in 1974 and for Fulham in
the 1970s, and though he wasn't the force he once
was then, in 1971 Georgie was at the same level as
Johan Cruyff and Franz Beckenbauer, with only
Pele above him. Also, the only European team I've
seen who have had an attacking trio as good as
Best, Charlton and Law at the same time was the
Barcelona team featuring Lionel Messi, Neymar
and Luis Suarez.

So, who was going to replace Malcolm
MacDonald? That short straw was given to the
barrel-chested Vic Halom. Vic was a bit hit and
miss for the Town, after joining from Fulham for
£35,000 early in the season. Though he was part of
something special in 1973...

The Town got off to a draw-laden start to 1971-72, with 6 draws coming in their first 7 League games. The other game they lost (2-1 at Burnley), as well as losing a League Cup tie at Crystal Palace, 2-0.

When the Hatters first win did come, it was a thrilling 3-2 victory against Middlesbrough at Kenilworth Road (Nobby Stiles and all). Halom netted, as did Robin Wainwright, who showed a lot of early promise, and Peter Anderson, who was to become a prolific scorer from midfield for the Town. Wainwright and Halom then scored again in a 2-0 home win over Fulham. But, just when it looked like Luton's goalscoring concerns post-MacDonald were decreasing, two goalless draws followed. A major worry for the Town board must also have been the low attendances. No gate reached 15,000 until the New Year's Day clash with Millwall.

Even Eric Morecambe wasn't always happy either. I was a member of the Junior Hatters at this time, and I saw Eric 'lose it' on one occasion at one of our dos. Rightly so, in truth, as some kids were playing up, and thinking that gentle Eric wouldn't say anything. You could have heard a pin drop after Eric's explosion and a sense of quiet bewilderment among the kids. We'd just seen Eric's light side on TV, but, if anything, he now gained even more respect from us.

The early Seventies was also a time when hooliganism was everywhere. Aspiring to be a 'boot boy' when I got older, when hordes of Charlton Athletic fans were pouring towards the Oak Road End from the Kenilworth Road end in November,

1971, I suddenly didn't find hooliganism so glamorous. I remember moving from the left of the Oak Road End ever nearer to the middle, as Charlton hoolies moved at pace through the then Bobbers Stand (now where the executive boxes are). Yes, even Charlton Athletic had a sizeable hooligan contingent. Every club had, it seemed, in 1971-72. Luton also lost the game 2-1!

A 3-2 victory over Portsmouth at home, after the Town had been 2-0 down, briefly lifted the gloom, as did the emergence of the promising young full-back Don Shanks. But, for Hatters fans, there were too many draws, too few goals, and too few home wins. A 2-0 win against Bristol City just before Christmas was to be their fourth of only seven home wins all season. But, great joy. Watford fared a lot worse. They finished bottom of the table with a pathetic 19 points - 5 wins, and only 24 goals scored. However, relegated Charlton won two more games than Luton's 10 wins all season.

1972 began with successive wins against Millwall (home) and Preston (away), before the Hatters were paired with West Ham United in the FA Cup at Upton Park - Bobby Moore, Geoff Hurst and all.

My Dad thought that he'd treat me to my first away game, and the Hatters played really well I thought. It was also the first game I'd ever been to with my Dad. West Ham's Clyde Best really caught my eye in the game, and he was the catalyst for the wave of gifted black players in English football that followed later in the decade. Tony Read saved a penalty from Geoff Hurst, but Luton just went down 2-1, and England's hat-trick hero of '66 did get on the scoresheet, along with Best. Don Givens netted for the Town, and Trevor Brooking, Billy Bonds, Frank Lampard Senior, Bryan 'Pop' Robson and Harry Redknapp appeared for the Hammers, alongside Hurst, Moore and Best. West Ham had beaten Man United in their previous League game at home 3-0, so it underlined Luton's gallant performance.

On the way to the match a particularly scary West Ham skinhead was waiting in an underground station looking for Luton victims. He just seemed a bit of an idiot all on his lonesome as we walked past him. Though, maybe he had just missed his train. Inside the ground, two West Ham fans around my age were amazed that we'd come all the way from Luton. We may as well as come from Mars! The crowd of 32,099 was the biggest I'd been amongst too.

A next door neighbour and playmate around this time was David Arnold. I'd hear him playing music through the wall, and then I saw much later that he wrote the score for *Independence Day*, scores for James Bond movies, the *Little Britain* theme, *et al*. Practice makes perfect obviously.

Also in the early '70s my friends and I would kick a ball about with Chris Lockwood, who played for the England Ladies team, and is remembered now as one of the Lost Lionesses. Luton, in fact, was the hotbed of women's football in England around this time. There'll be more on Chris in my *Made in Luton* project, with updates on my paulrance.com website.

It was back to harsh reality the following weekend, as the Town went down 3-1 at Fulham in front of 11,328. It was the start of a dismal run in the League of no wins in 7 games, two home defeats, and which culminated in a 0-0 home draw with Watford. Such was the disenchantment of Hatters fans by this time, and with Hornets fans even more depressed, only 10,816 turned up for the derby at Kenilworth Road in early March.

For the next home game, against Burnley, the attendance dipped below 9,000 for the first time all season. But a little brainchild of mine before the match was to create an Oak Road-like atmosphere at the Kenilworth Road End. So, along with some mates, we congregated at a corner of Kenilworth Road to create an atmosphere - and to intimidate Burnley fans. We were 12 years old after all...

I seem to remember that there were about a dozen of us, but, under the influence of alcohol, and, depending on my mood, it could have been as many as 30, or as little as 5 or 6. The Burnley fans were good natured, and so we left them alone. Luton won the game 1-0, thanks to a Viv Busby goal. At the previous home game, Chris Nicholl had scored his last goal in a Luton shirt in a 2-1 defeat to Sunderland. Luton's player of the season for 1970-71 was sold shortly afterwards to Aston Villa. So, in less than a year, Luton's two biggest playing assets, Malcolm MacDonald and Chris Nicholl, had gone. Alan Garner, a signing from Millwall, was then given his chance as Nicholl's replacement.

Talking of Millwall... I did go along to the odd reserve game in my early years as a Town supporter, which I recall usually watching from the Maple Road stand. Though you were free to move around, such was the sparse nature of the crowds. Anyway, Luton 4 Millwall 2 was a reserve game I saw in late March, and my team-sheet (no programme) has Luton players such as Charlie Sorbie and Gerry Jones (who scored one of Luton's goals) on it. A young Paul Price also played.

Vic Halom also scored in that Midweek Football

League Cup game, and he finally delivered for the Town first team a few days later, as his 12 minute hat-trick helped the Hatters defeat Sheffield Wednesday 3-1 at Kenilworth Road. The sub-10,000 crowds at home continued, however, and the Hatters board must have been envious of the 34,349 crowd the Town had played in front of at Birmingham City a week earlier. A 1-0 defeat against a side bound for Division One was also hardly as lamentable as some performances, such as against Blackpool at home...

Luton followed up their Easter Saturday victory over the Owls with a 1-0 home defeat to Hull. But the real nadir, on the pitch, of the 1971-72 season was a 4-1 spanking at Kenilworth Road by Blackpool. 3-0 down at half-time, Alan Slough scored an own goal, and my remarks on the back of the match programme stated that "Luton were well and truly thrashed today". I also remarked that Keith Dyson missed an absolute sitter for the Tangerines. Mike Keen scored his last goal for us in this game, and it was obvious that the side needed a major shake-up. With the strikers misfiring all season, now even the defence was looking shaky without Chris Nicholl's commanding presence. Many of the 7,270 who turned up were hardly being enticed to come back.

But, Luton being Luton, in their next game they pulled off an unlikely 3-0 win at Portsmouth. John Ryan scored twice to show the strikers how to do it. No more victories followed, and the last home game was, appropriately for a damp squib of a season, a 0-0 draw with Bristol City. It was also Alec Stock's last home game in charge of the Town, and, overall, he'd been successful. He'd also moulded the likes of MacDonald and Nicholl into top class players. The Paul Whitehouse character, Ron Manager from *The Fast Show*, was, by Whitehouse's own admission, largely based on Alec Stock. A bit harsh, as I don't remember Alec like that, or him ever mentioning "jumpers for goalposts"!

Among the other departures from Kenilworth Road were skipper Mike Keen, who had been a great captain for the club, and who had been a dependable player for Alec Stock when he had managed QPR. Unspectacular, Mike was similar to Brian Horton in that respect, but, like Horton, he got the best out of the more gifted players around him. The trouble was, in 1971-72, Luton were lacking in quality, and the side also needed some younger legs in Keen's position.

Like Keen, David Court was given a free transfer. Court had been a regular, and Keen an ever-present in the League in 1971-72, so the Luton midfield was having a major overhaul. It was also reported at the time that David Court had to sign on, because no club wanted him. Yes, modern footballers earn too much in relation to their talent. But, nowadays, at least a footballer who has been at a club in the top two divisions for a few years shouldn't need to worry about benefits. That seems right, but in the '70s George Best would have been earning probably the equivalent of what a mediocre Premier League player earns now - if that.

Don Givens also left the Hatters, and he was sold to QPR. It didn't seem such a big loss at the time, because Don only scored 8 League goals all season (three of which had been penalties), and he was an ever-present in the League. But, among better players at QPR, including the likes of Stan Bowles and Gerry Francis, Don Givens was going to flourish and become a key part of QPR's greatest-ever team.

The '71-'72 season had been a bit of a let down. After two promotions and a couple of near misses in the previous four seasons, Luton fans experienced that rare thing - a mainly dull season.

So, with the manager gone, three first team regulars on their way, a rebuild was gonna be happening. That the players that came into the club probably exceeded most Hatters fans expectations would be an understatement. Before all that I picked up some autographs at a six-a-side tournament in late April at Kenilworth Road. Namely, DJ Pete Murray, Alan Garner, and 'keeper Keith Barber. Eric Morecambe was also involved in the Show Biz 6, with Murray, and they drew 5-5 with Barton Rovers. Rovers won on corners - now there's a new way of settling a drawn cup tie! Mike Keen and Don Givens were in a Luton Town B side, and so this was their last Town appearance at Kenilworth Road. A Town new boy, John Faulkner, was also in the B side.

1972-73 - Harry, Great Signings and Cup Heartbreak

John Faulkner was among a number of impressive Hatters signings, before the 1972-73 season, and having played for the mighty Leeds United meant that he should find Division 2 football a breeze. Luton also shelled out a club record £50,000 to sign the Leicester City forward who'd impressed me so much two years earlier - Rodney Fern. But, the two signings that staggered me were John Aston and Bobby Thomson.

Aston had been a member of Manchester United's European Cup winning side just four years earlier, and had been on the opposite wing to George Best at Wembley when United became the first English club to be crowned European champions. After playing his part in the 4-1 defeat of Benfica, four years on Aston was now going to be one of our star players!

Left-back Thomson was another big signing.

Capped by England 8 times in the mid-1960s (the outstanding Ray Wilson, probably England's greatest left-back of all-time, happened to be, unfortunately for Bobby, around at the same time), Thomson's signing from Birmingham gave Luton a fine leader and steadying influence at the back. With Alan Garner and 'keeper Keith Barber looking promising, Alan Slough, John Moore and John Ryan reliable, plus the newly arrived John Faulkner and Thomson, Luton's defensive options were now looking good.

Peter Anderson had been Luton's top scorer in 1971-72, with 10 goals from midfield, and with wingers Jimmy Ryan and John Aston, allied to the arrival of Fern, there looked more of a goal threat now. Viv Busby, it was hoped, would also kick on, after a traumatic loan spell at Newcastle in '71-'72, when he and Supermac came unstuck at Hereford in the FA Cup!

Commercial manager Harry Haslam was the surprise choice to replace Alec Stock, and Roy McCrohan became his assistant, replacing Jimmy Andrews. I knew both Harry and Roy's sons at Icknield High School. I didn't have any problems with Harry's son Keith (unlike Mansfield Town fans decades later!), but I remember Roy's son Andy once saying to me, "I hate you, Rance." Blimey, what did I do! First time I'd ever been hated! Anyway, Harry and Roy were a good partnership, and Harry's contacts had proved useful in landing John Aston - Harry was a friend of John's Dad, John Aston Senior, and that couldn't have done any harm when it came to getting John Junior to sign for Luton. Harry had been sacked on the same day as

Bobby Robson, then manager of Fulham, but before he left the Cottagers Haslam had noticed a young talent called Malcolm Macdonald. So, the new Town manager seemed to be able to identify young players who had star quality.

My parents had met Harry Haslam and his wife Trudi at an event at Cardinal Newman School. They seemed nice, unaffected people, and some of the Town players were also at the event. I remember my Mother telling me that Ken Goodeve was a charming fella...

The 1972-73 season seemed like a new era. New manager, a lot of personnel changes in the team, and, of course, the debut of the famous orange shirt - initially for away games, and the not so attractive new badge that consisted of just "Lt" in a football, with "Luton Town Football Club" around it. In the pre-season team photo, and almost as notable, can be seen the impressive moustaches Alan Slough and Derek Hales are sporting.

Bobby Thomson, John Faulkner, Rodney Fern and John Aston all started in Luton's first game of the season at Cardiff (ironically the Town's last game of the '71-'72 season had been a 1-1 draw at Cardiff). But, though Aston netted a penalty, the Town lost 2-1. It was also an established figure, Peter Anderson, who earnt the most praise from Peter Jackson of *the South Wales Echo*!

Luton won their next two games 1-0, and hammered Huddersfield Town 4-1 in their fifth - following a 1-0 defeat at Oxford. Vic Halom scored a couple against the Terriers, with Aston again scoring from the spot. While Jimmy Ryan scored the other Hatters goal. At this stage of the season Luton had a very bold formation, with Halom, Rodney Fern, Viv Busby (as the three strikers), Aston and Ryan (on the flanks) all being in the same side.

Vic Halom commented that Luton's more attacking style under Haslam should mean at least 15 goals apiece in the season from him, and from Busby, Fern and Peter Anderson too!

Luton seemed to be thriving under Haslam, and followed up their victory over Huddersfield with a fine 1-1 draw at St. Andrew's against Birmingham City in the League Cup. A 1-0 win at Nottingham Forest followed and Luton lay 6th in the Division 2 table after 6 games.

The Luton-Birmingham League Cup tie stretched to three games, but the first replay at Kenilworth Road should have seen the Town triumph. John Aston put the Hatters ahead midway through the second-half, but City's Alan Campbell scored with two minutes left to take the game into extra-time. Not good for me, as my Dad was waiting to pick me up, and, as I've said, he wasn't the biggest footie fan. Dad asked a cheerful Town fan next to me how long there was to go, as my Father had decided to wait inside the ground. The guy said: "Thirty minutes." Dad's grumpy response: "Bloody football." The words 'ground', 'swallow', 'me', and 'up' came to mind. To complete a bizarre evening, my Dad's best mate at school, and Syd Owen's understudy, Terry Kelly, was featured in the match programme. The match finished 1-1.

Luton's form continued to be good, as they won 2-1 at home to Brighton in the League, before finally being defeated by a late Trevor Francis goal in the second League Cup replay against Birmingham, which was at St. Andrew's.

The Town seemed to have a League Cup hangover three days later as Sheffield Wednesday hammered the Hatters 4-0 at Hillsborough. With a midfield and forward line of Anderson, Aston, Jimmy Ryan, Fern, Busby and Halom the Town defence was not offered much protection against a side scoring goals for fun at home. A brace by Vic Halom put Luton back on track at Swindon, and Luton's young Irish 'keeper Willie Carrick kept a clean sheet on his debut in a 2-0 win.

Burnley were next up, and the Kenilworth Road choir experiment was repeated. While, with a rare visit by the *Match of the Day* cameras, it gave us even more of a reason to make ourselves heard. The Kenilworth Road pitch was eye-catching for the Beeb, with a circular pattern inspiring a young Leighton James it seemed to make his name with two goals for the visitors. The game was a thriller between two teams looking likely to be in the promotion mix come the end of the season. A week later and there was another 2-2 home draw against Lancashire opposition. This time, Blackpool. Young Blackpool 'keeper John Burridge denied Luton all the points with a great save from Viv Busby in the last minute. Incredibly, Luton also drew their next home game 2-2 against Portsmouth, and future Town goalkeeper Graham Horn was between the sticks for Pompey.

Sandwiched between the Blackpool and Portsmouth games was a trip to Sunderland at Roker Park. The Hatters won 2-0, with Rodney Fern in inspired form, but Town fans would have happily swapped this score with the Black Cats in the League, for a different FA Cup result later in the season...

There's not much wrong with Luton's away form, but their home form looks like it could prove to be costly. They lie fourth after 16 games, but with only three home wins, and one of their two home defeats is to Hull. Against the Tigers Luton again concede two goals, and they go down 2-1. A 1-0 win at Bristol City follows, but the Hatters flop again in their next home game, a 1-0 defeat to Swindon, and then again at home to Carlisle 1-0.

Remarkably, Luton's away form is a polar opposite to their home form. The Town draw at Portsmouth, shock a near 30,000 crowd at Villa Park with a 2-0 victory against Aston Villa, thanks to goals from Fern and Aston, and then win 1-0 at Middlesbrough. Bruce Rioch and Chris Nicholl are in the defeated Villa side.

Luton, though, don't win again in the League at home until January, when they beat Forest 1-0. Included in this winless sequence of 10 games is FIVE 2-2 draws in 8 matches! Two bright spots in the gloom were Barry Butlin, who scored on his Town debut against QPR at Kenilworth Road (Don Givens scored for Rangers in a 2-2 draw), and, a week later, the return of Town legend Graham French against Millwall in another 2-2 draw at home in mid-December.

After being involved in a robbery and subsequently imprisoned, French made other so-called bad boys in football look rather tame - if you believe all you read in the papers. Which I probably did at the time. Graham went out with the daughter of a friend of my Mother's, and I never heard anything bad about him. Graham French hadn't played for the Town for three years, so his comeback seemed a bit unreal - more so that he actually scored. Unfortunately, French's comeback could never reach the heights of his career of the late 1960s, when he was up there with Bruce Rioch as Luton's most gifted player.

Even more unreal in 1973 was Luton's FA Cup run. A 2-0 home win against Crewe in the 3rd Round gave Town fans their first home victory for exactly 4 months. Next, a 2-1 win at Huddersfield gave Luton their 8th away win in the League, before they beat Forest a week later for their first home League win since September 13th! At Huddersfield, Luton had played in front of just 3,871.

I was staying at my maternal Grandparents in Barton-le-Clay the weekend Luton took on Newcastle up at St. James' Park. It was the 4th Round of the FA Cup, and Malcolm MacDonald being in the Magpies line-up gave the game even more significance. As the Geordies had gone out to Hereford the previous season, and Luton's away record was exceptional, a Luton win wouldn't have been so big a shock. But, when it came, to a 13-year-old like me it was stunning. Two John Aston goals in front of over 42,000 was the best result for me so far as a Hatters fan. So, my visit to my Grandparents was more fun than usual. We'd beaten a team from the First Division, after some near misses, and that was a really big deal.

A rare away defeat, at Brighton, followed the Newcastle game, before it was back to usual - another home draw. However, the 1-1 draw against Cardiff did give me the chance to be on TV for the first time. I was by the corner flag in the Oak Road End, near the Bobbers Stand, and so it was a safe bet I'd be on the box. None of this daft, modern waving stuff when the cameras were on me though... Derek Hales also scored his first and last goal for the Hatters in this game.

But Luton's stuttering League form could be forgiven, as the Town were three games away from Wembley, and nearly 40,000 saw an Alan Garner header secure victory against Bolton Wanderers at Burnden Park in the 5th Round of the FA Cup. It was to be Sunderland in the quarter-finals, but neither the Town or the Black Cats could win the FA Cup, could they? After all, a Division Two side hadn't won the trophy since 1931.

A friend of my Dad's was a big Sunderland fan. He seemed quite confident, when he came to see us, that the Black Cats could win the whole thing. Poor, deluded fool...

Two winless away games came after the Bolton game, then, as fate often dictates, Sunderland visited Kenilworth Road a week before the cup game. A Don Shanks goal was enough for a Hatters victory and to give us a League double against Sunderland for the season.

A staggering 53,156 turned up for the quarter-final

(50,000+ attendances were rare for any team in 1972-73) between Sunderland and Luton - around 40,000 more than for the League game at Roker Park five months earlier! Vic Halom was also now in the red and white stripes of Sunderland after his move to the North East giants.

I'd never cried over a Luton defeat up to this point. But, we'd won at Newcastle, then at the eventual Division 3 champions Bolton, so, on paper, average Sunderland looked the less difficult game of the three. Football doesn't work like that, of course, and we crashed out 2-0, and the tears flowed.

Sunderland then went on to beat the greatest team in English football at the time in the FA Cup final, Leeds United, and it was the greatest FA Cup final shock result in history. I cried again. It could have been us, but I also got very emotionally involved in Sunderland's victory just because it was a footballing fairytale. "Wonderland!" *The Mirror* exclaimed. In truth, Sunderland had punched very low below their weight in the League. Dave Watson, Dennis Tueart, Jim Montgomery, Billy Hughes, Bobby Kerr and Ian Porterfield (the scorer of the final's only goal) would all have graced good Division One sides, let alone a mid-table Division Two one. Watson became an England regular, and Tueart also became an England international and one of the game's biggest stars. Vic Halom, then, found himself playing in an FA Cup final and picking up a winners medal. Still, we had Barry Butlin now, and that was more than enough compensation for losing Halom, though he had been having a fine season for the Town.

Bristol City were in town a week after the Sunderland defeat. Just over 7,000 showed up to see a depressing 3-1 defeat (I left early, and I saw some Bristol City greasers hanging around on their motorbikes looking for trouble), and a 1-0 win at Fulham soon after didn't really lift the spirits of many Luton fans. No Wembley dreams left, and a wish to see the season end early. A promising start in the League had just seen the Town's home form deteriorate to that of a team relegation bound.

Alec Stock was back in Town as Fulham manager in early April, and Luton secured a narrow victory. A 2-0 win at QPR was one outstanding result late in the season, as that side was on the way to promotion. QPR were also on the verge of being one of the best teams in the country, with Stan Bowles, Gerry Francis, Phil Parkes, Dave Thomas and Don Givens all starring in a Rangers side that were Division 1 runners-up just three years later. Givens was the top scorer in Division 2 in 1972-73, with 23 goals, and few Hatters fans saw that coming when he hadn't reached double figures in the League with us in 1971-72!

For the final home game of the season it was a chance to see dear old Nobby Stiles play for Middlesbrough. His England replacement Alan Mullery had been in the Fulham side at Luton shortly before. At this point I hadn't missed a home League game for two-and-a-half years. The trouble was I had recently ruptured my gut (as painful as it sounds), and I was nearly keeling over as I held on to a Kenilworth Road crash barrier for dear life. It was also a hot day in late April, and I was getting funny looks from people as I realised I should have stayed at home - and Boro won 1-0. But 1973-74 was going to be an interesting season, with three promotion places up for grabs to Division 1, and if Luton could get their home form sorted out, who knows?

1973-74 - In the Big Time!

No clutch of new signings and a 4-0 hammering at Nottingham Forest on the opening day of the season meant that even I was beginning to lose interest. The Gillette Cup final was live on TV when the Hatters played their first home game - against Carlisle. I chose to watch the cricket, and so miss my first home League game since the middle of the 1970-71 season. I looked at the half-time scores, and I didn't know whether to laugh or cry. It was Luton SIX Carlisle 0. So, I'm now living in Roman Road in Leagrave, and thinking: "I could get to the ground in half-an-hour, and so catch much of the second-half." But I thought that Luton probably wouldn't score, and so compound my sense of disbelief. I'd never seen Luton score six before, let alone in one half. It finished 6-1, and, not for the first time, I'd picked the wrong game to miss... A famous name, Tom Finney, scored twice on his full Town debut. But, this Tom Finney was an Irish guy.

Finney scored again in a 3-1 win at Bristol City, in a 1-1 draw at Notts County, and in the 3-3 thriller with Portsmouth at home. Defenders Bobby Thomson and Alan Garner also got rare goals in that game. Four successive League wins followed, and Luton were, unexpectedly, near the top of the table in mid-October. The run had started with a bit of revenge - a 1-0 win at Sunderland, thanks to a Barry Butlin goal. Butlin then got two more in a 3-0 win over Blackpool at Kenilworth Road, and he netted again at Crystal Palace. It was the 2-1 win against Palace, a team that had been playing First Division football the season before, that had Hatters fans believing that this could be a big season.

No notable signings had been made for a while, which had made Luton's good start so surprising. Then, when the Town splashed out a record £100,000 on Burnley midfielder Alan West in October, it looked like the club was really going for it. Westie made his debut in a 2-0 defeat at Orient, but it was Luton's first defeat in 11 League and cup games.

The Town's reserve side was also riding high in the Football Combination (though the Town were bottom in the Mid-Week League in mid-November). While Rodney Fern was soon in double figures, and Peter Cruse scored 7 goals in his first 5 games in the FC. Notable results included a 7-1 win at Ipswich, which followed a 5-1 win at home to QPR.

In the Second Division, Luton had been in second place in the table, but they hit a mini slump in form, which saw them fall down to eighth. The Town let a 2-0 lead slip at home to Hull to draw 2-2. I wrote about Peter Anderson at the time that he "must be the best midfielder in Division Two." A goal against Hull in late October had him on 5 League goals already.

One amusing memory of Hull City fans in the '70s was being nervous that they were about to come near my home, which was two miles from Kenilworth Road! I could hear them chanting "Yorkshire!" at the top of Chester Avenue, just a few hundred yards from Roman Road. But, it seemed more a case that they'd just got lost, so we put the barricades away. The chant also seemed to be a political one, as Hull became part of the new regional Humberside authority in the '70s.

Middlesbrough had got off to a storming start under new boss Jack Charlton, when the Town arrived at Ayresome Park in early November. It was a biggie even this early in the season, and a 2-1 defeat didn't seem the end of the world, as Boro looked like running away with the division.

Another rare defeat came in the League Cup 4th Round at Millwall, but in early December the Town were, joy of joys, still unbeaten at home. That run ended with a 2-0 defeat by West Brom, but the missing link in the Luton jigsaw, Jimmy Husband, made his debut for the club in that game after signing from Everton.

The lights went out on the Town during their 1-0 win at home to Cardiff in mid-December (these were the '70s and the days of regular power cuts), and then a 1-0 home win against Aston Villa put Luton fans in great spirits just before Christmas.

Ex-Hatters Chris Nicholl and Neil Rioch were in the Villa side, and soon-to-be ex-England manager Alf Ramsey looked on from the main stand. The then three-day week must also have affected programme printing, as the programmes for the Fulham and Bristol City games consisted of just 8 pages each! Games were also kicking off early (2pm) because of floodlight issues...

Two successive away defeats - at Blackpool (a 3-0 stuffing three days before Christmas) and at Carlisle on New Year's Day didn't do the Town too much damage, as they remained in the top three. While, in an FA Cup 3rd Round replay at home to Port Vale, Peter Anderson scored two goals as a no. 9 in place of the absent Barry Butlin and Jimmy Husband. Jimmy Ryan was also finding good goalscoring form - helped by his being on penalty duty. Jimmy netted a pen in a 2-2 home draw with Forest, with the mercurial Duncan McKenzie scoring one of the Forest goals.

A little bit of history occurred in Luton's 4th Round FA Cup tie against Bradford City, in late January at Kenilworth Road. The Town took the lead after just 15 seconds, as the appropriately named David Fretwell scored the quickest own goal in English professional football ever! The Bantams went down 3-0.

A 1-0 win at Aston Villa kept Luton in third spot, but a 1-1 home draw with Notts County disappointed most of the Kenilworth Road crowd that actually did turn up. Just 4,908 did, as, with power cuts still an issue, the game was played on a Tuesday afternoon! But, for the FA Cup 5th Round home tie against First Division Leicester City, 25,712 turned up to watch Peter Shilton, Frank Worthington, Keith Weller, Alan Birchenall and co.

Keith Weller scored the goal of the season in that game, which involved his waltzing past the Town defence. Frank Worthington also scored, as the Town were hammered 4-0 by a classy top flight outfit.

Around this time we had a new arrival in the family - a female black cat called Lucky. When my Mother took her to the vet on the bus, the bus inspector hoped "she'd bring the Town some luck". Little did he know...

In the next 10 days the Leicester defeat was made up for with successive League wins against Palace and Swindon. On March 16th, and just after a notable 3-1 win at Hull, Luton hosted Orient in the Town's biggest League game of the season so far. Luton had climbed to second in the table after the Swindon victory, and were still there when the Londoners arrived. Orient were breathing down the Hatters neck though, and 17,045 turned up to see a Jimmy Husband hat-trick secure a 3-1 win. Middlesbrough were out of sight at the top, but Luton were now in pole position to take one of the two remaining promotion places. Even successive 1-0 defeats didn't dent Luton's hopes, and one of those defeats was at home to all-conquering Middlesbrough.

Boro created a post-War record for the Second Division, with their points tally of 65, and it wasn't hard to see why. Their defence was one of the best

Division Two had ever seen, and in midfield and attack there was the emerging Graeme Souness and David Armstrong, experienced quality in the shape of Bobby Murdoch and John Hickton, and a player who was to become British football's first £500,000 signing - David Mills. It was Mills who scored the only goal of the game at Kenilworth Road in front of just under 20,000.

A 4-2 win at home to Preston, with a hat-trick from Luton's best no. 9 since Supermac, Barry Butlin, followed the Boro defeat. The Preston win turned out to be vital, as Luton then failed to win their next three games.

The first of those games, a 1-1 draw at Oxford, was my first trip to an away game in the League. A friend (he shall remain nameless) was sick at the back of the coach (lucky we weren't going to Carlisle), and my friend Simon Mayles and I led the Oak Road End as we marched towards the Manor Ground. This wasn't anything to do with bravado - we just happened to be there first. There was some aggro, or "A-G, A-G-R, A-G-R-O, AGGRO!" - as was the popular chant of the day when things were about to kick off. It was a surprise to see Oxford hooligans looking for trouble, because I thought the Manor Ground would be one of the safer grounds to visit. But, as I've already said, it seemed like every club had its hooligan element - even if it was just to protect their own patch and nothing else.

In the match itself, a freakish Jimmy Ryan free-kick from 40 yards helped earn the Town a point. But Luton have had a habit of faltering over Easter, and that Good Friday game at Oxford was followed by a

2-2 draw at Sheffield Wednesday, and a 1-0 defeat to Oxford in the return fixture. So, just two points out of a possible six at Easter then - but still we remained second.

A 3-0 triumph over Millwall at Kenilworth Road then set things up for promotion at West Brom the following Saturday. Just a point required!

I went up to the Hawthorns with an old friend - Clive Ayres. The whole day was an experience, and my best day as a Hatters fan at that time. The game was, I believe, also the first live match a little West Brom supporter ever saw - future TV and radio presenter Adrian Chiles.

Before the game a guy showed Clive and I an FA Cup final ticket for that year. Then, it was like someone showing you Moon rock or something, and our eyes were on stalks. Jeez, we'd actually seen an FA Cup final ticket.

Luton seemed pretty nerveless in the game, and the ever dependable Barry Butlin put us ahead. Then I had my first bad experience with police at a football match - courtesy of the West Midlands Police Force. Hatters fans were jumping up and down - with joy. Well, one grizzled old cop decided that he didn't like that, and he went wading in, striking as many Town fans as he could with a stick and not a truncheon. The cop's young colleague thought that he'd do the same, but he got beaten up by Hatters fans. I thought at the time that he'd been beaten unconscious, but he must have got out of there somehow. The grizzled old cop had too much nous to risk getting some of the same. It was all grim, and threatened to put a damper on the day, and then West Brom equalised.

Luton hung on, and it was one of those 'pinch me' moments. We were in the First Division. You see, there was the perception at the time that we were 'little Luton', and so First Division football was just a silly fantasy for a club like ours. Perhaps, more remarkably, Carlisle United came up with us to be in the top flight for the first time. So, maybe being 6-0 down in a game at half-time early on in a campaign doesn't need to define your season...

At the final whistle at the Hawthorns we tried to get onto the pitch to celebrate. But, the cops were pushing fans back, regardless of them potentially injuring themselves on the concrete terracing. I'd never been so angry at a game, and it's the only time I can remember swearing at cops at a match. It kinda seemed that the police couldn't bear to see 'little' old us getting promoted, while mighty West Brom were stuck in the middle of Division Two.

The Town finished runners-up. Just a mere 15 points behind Middlesbrough, but who cared. Carlisle were the first Second Division club to benefit from three going up, as they finished a point behind our tally of 50.

On the coach home we heard on the radio, with some incredulity, that Luton had replaced Manchester United in the First Division. A bitter-sweet moment. We'd loved to have played United, but to be a division above them seemed unthinkable then, let alone now! While I remember when I first started getting into football that many kids in Luton supported United (they were the kids favourite big club in fact), rather than their home town team. Yes, ironic indeed, and I'd like to think that children in Manchester and Surrey in '74 chucked in their allegiance to United, and switched it to the Town instead. I know, I know, unlikely...

Luton's last game of the season was at home, and it couldn't have been against a better opponent - FA Cup winners Sunderland. The Black Cats spoiled the promotion party a tad, but, in truth, it seemed more like a testimonial game. Sunderland won 4-3, with Vic Halom netting the winner. 20,285 were there to enjoy the party.

The Town side didn't seem to have a weakness - at Division 2 level anyway. A young Graham Horn had emerged as a fine 'keeper, and John Ryan, Bobby Thomson, John Faulkner and Alan Garner were all dependable. Peter Anderson and Alan West were two classy midfielders, and Jimmy Ryan and John Aston were as good a pair of wide men as there was in the division. Barry Butlin was probably the Town's player of the season, and his strike partnership with Jimmy Husband really flourished in the latter stages of the campaign.

The Town's regular line-up for '73-'74 was: Graham Horn; Don Shanks/John Ryan (Ryan was a regular all season, but he only played at right-back in the second-half of the season, when he replaced Shanks in that position), Bobby Thomson, John Faulkner, Alan Garner; Peter Anderson, Alan West, Jimmy Ryan, John Aston; Jimmy Husband, Barry Butlin.

1974-75 - The Anti-Climax

Luton had a new song for Division 1 - *Hatters, Hatters* by The Barron Knights. Not as enduring as Chelsea's *Blue Is the Colour*, but catchy enough. The line "Never Again Division Two" was, though, tempting fate...

Hatters fans looked forward to the fixture list more than usual, of course, for '74-'75, and when the fixture list did come out the first game couldn't have been much bigger - FA Cup holders Liverpool at home. Though Luton's first game in Division One since 1960 was made all-ticket, so it was gonna be a trip to Kenilworth Road and back twice! I wasn't happy, as I suspected the ground wouldn't quite have reached its 31,000 capacity anyway (yes, 31,000 - and I remember thinking that we'd never be a big club with a titchy capacity like that).

August the 17th was the day Kevin Keegan, Ray Clemence and the Reds came to Town, and the hype was even bigger than when the fixtures came out - because of Keegan's infamous brawl with Leeds Billy Bremner at Wembley a week earlier. At the Charity Shield pre-League season showcase, both Keegan and Bremner had been sent off. The match at Kenilworth Road was also Bob Paisley's first League game in charge of the Reds, after Bill Shankly surprisingly decided to retire. Good luck trying to match or surpass Shanks' achievements, Bob...

Barry Butlin put the Town ahead, but Liverpool came back to win 2-1. The Hatters had still been impressive though, as there weren't going to be many stiffer tests than Liverpool. Ray Clemence also showed his good humour, when one guy on the Kenilworth Road terrace shouted at the Liverpool & England 'keeper: "Call yourself a goalkeeper, Clemence?" Ray turned round and smiled, and just said: "Yeah!" Kevin Keegan, ever emotional, threatened to quit football after the game, because of Town fans taunting him with "Keegan - Bremner" chants. The 21,062 crowd was a decent attendance, but its being all-ticket obviously deterred some.

A 2-0 defeat at West Ham was a more troubling loss, and Alan Garner was withdrawn through injury. This left John Ryan as one of the Town's centre-halves for the next few games. John Faulkner and Jimmy Ryan also had injury problems early in the season, and Gordon Hindson (for Jimmy Ryan) was given a run of games. Geordie Hindson had been on the fringes at Luton for several seasons, but he had rarely let the Town down in the games he did play. Don Shanks also came back into the side at right-back, as the injury woes continued. It was no coincidence that, when Luton had few injury problems in '73-'74, they got promoted, but were soon struggling in Division One when the successful side was severely disrupted. Physio Reg Game certainly had his hands full.

A 1-1 draw at Middlesbrough was more like it, but a 0-0 home draw against West Ham was disappointing. The Hammers had a useful side (they went on to win the FA Cup that season), with Trevor Brooking, Billy Bonds, Clyde Best and Frank Lampard Senior in their line-up. But it was becoming clear that the Town were going to have to beat 'useful' sides at home to survive in Division One. The man in black at the West Ham game was another notable name, Clive 'the Book' Thomas. He even cautioned me for looking at him funny...

In the next home game, against QPR, new signing Adrian Alston made his Hatters debut. Dubbed 'Socceroo', Alston had also played for Australia in the recent World Cup in West Germany, including against the hosts and eventual world champions.

Luton could only draw with QPR, but a 1-1 draw at reigning champions Leeds United was a great result - regardless of new manager Brian Clough's problems with getting the likes of Billy Bremner and Johnny Giles to believe in him. This was Cloughie's last game in charge of Leeds, and it was a Barry Butlin header that did for him. Yes, a header. The Clough biopic *The Damned United* had Luton scoring through a shot.

Luton's first win of the season came in a League

Cup tie at home to Bristol Rovers, before a brutal 4-1 hammering by Ipswich Town at Kenilworth Road. Bobby Robson was putting together a fine side at Portman Road, and Luton felt its full force - but at least Alston netted his first Town goals in those two games.

The Town were doing okay away from home at this stage, as was underlined by a 2-2 draw at Arsenal in late September. Alston scored for the third game running, and Don Shanks grabbed a rare goal. I went to this game at Highbury with the Mayles family, who are lifetime family friends. I remember Cynthia, Mother of Simon, having a go at some Arsenal fan who was leaning all over us. The pre-match entertainment seemed quite quaint, with some old guy singing. A couple of days later he was on ITV's *Today* programme saying that he thought some of the players didn't acknowledge his mellifluous tones. He'd been singing at Highbury for years apparently.

An irritating aspect of Luton in '74-'75 was the Town's propensity to be unpredictable. Successive away draws at Middlesbrough, Leeds and Arsenal should have meant a positive result at struggling Coventry was on the cards. But the Town went down 2-1, and, worst still, Barry Butlin was sold to Nottingham Forest.

Just under 13,000 turned up to watch the Hatters play Carlisle. The Cumbrians had started the season like a Ray Train (a pun for older footie fans), winning their first three League games in the top flight. But they were dropping like a stone by the time they arrived at Kenilworth Road in late

September. If the Town didn't win this game it seemed like they had had it already. Thankfully, the Hatters won 3-1. Alston scored again, Peter Anderson grabbed his first of the season, and Jimmy Ryan got his second in successive games.

A goalless draw at Filbert Street, against a Leicester side that had ripped Luton to shreds months earlier, was another notable result. While even a 2-0 away defeat at Sheffield United in the League Cup didn't seem too much to worry about - Division One survival was the main priority. After 11 games Luton were above a bottom three of Arsenal, Spurs and Chelsea! The Town were fifth from bottom at this stage, on 8 points. But, incredibly, the team just below the Town, Birmingham City, then struck the Hatters a huge blow at Kenilworth Road. Two goals from Trevor Francis and another from future Town star Bob Hatton left the Hatters deep in the mire.

Successive 1-0 defeats - at home to Boro and at Manchester City - meant that the Spurs game was a crucial match. A 1-1 draw at home to Spurs was better than nothing, but a 1-0 defeat at Newcastle left the Town bottom in early November. The Newcastle loss triggered a run of six League defeats in a row. In mid-December the Town were six points adrift at the bottom and things seemed hopeless. New names were coming into the side, such as Brian Chambers in midfield, Peter Spiring up front, and Steve Buckley at left-back. Even the almost forgotten Rodney Fern came back into the team briefly. Steve Litt had an extended run in the side, because of the injuries to Garner and Faulkner, and Keith Barber and Graham Horn were challenging each other for the goalkeeper's jersey.

But in amongst all the changes a diamond emerged - Paul Futcher.

Harry Haslam had signed 17-year-old twins Paul and Ron Futcher from Chester in the summer of '74. Pretty much identical twins at that. But no one really expected either to play this season because of their age, and because of their inexperience when it came to playing in the higher divisions. But things were getting desperate, and Paul was thrown in at the deep end at Stamford Bridge in early December. After playing in the 2-0 defeat against Chelsea, Paul also played in the next game, a 2-0 reverse against Liverpool at Anfield. Paul's home debut finally bought the Town some luck, and a 1-0 win over eventual League champions Derby County, thanks to a John Ryan goal, proved that Luton could beat one of the 'big boys'. Bruce Rioch was now starring for the Rams, alongside Francis Lee, Archie Gemmill and Colin Todd, who finished his playing career at Luton.

Then, on Boxing Day, Ron Futcher came in for his full debut and scored the only goal of the game in a stunning win at Ipswich. Ipswich had won 9 of their 11 home games at this point and were going for the title - though that particular race was wide open, with Middlesbrough, Stoke City, West Ham and Burnley all serious contenders. Ron's goal had given Bobby Robson's side a taste of defeat at home for the first time in the League that season. I also remember Paul Futcher saying after the game that Ipswich were "stereotyped". Firstly, I had to look the word up, and, secondly, I was staggered that an 18-year-old, with four Division One games under his belt, could put down one of the best teams in the country! But Luton needed that sort of cockiness I felt.

Town fans were beginning to believe again, and a 3-2 win at home to Wolves made it three League wins in a row over the Christmas period. 19,642 came and they saw Ron Futcher get a hat-trick. The Futcher twins had made an instant impact, and then some. Suddenly, they were being seen as the Town's saviours. Paul Futcher was being compared to Bobby Moore, and Ron Futcher had scored 4 in his first two full games. It would be hard to find any teenager in the previous ten years who'd made such an immediate impact in Division One as Paul and Ron - and Harry was looking a bit of a genius for signing 'em.

The New Year started badly for me. Just before the Birmingham City FA Cup game my maternal Grandfather had been taken ill. I thought that going to the 3rd Round tie at Kenilworth Road would distract me from distressing thoughts. But I just watched the game in a daze, and I felt sick every time the tannoy announcer began with: "Would..." Luton lost 1-0.

My Grandad died overnight. He had fuelled my love for the Hatters, with tales of Ernie Simms and Bob Hawkes (or maybe Fred?!), and memories of the famous 4-3 win over Newcastle in the 1940s. Grandad stopped going to matches after Luton got promoted for the first time to the top flight in 1955, and his daughter, my Mother Thelma, got married to my Dad Peter Rance later in the same year. Their reception at The Warden Tavern was overseen by its proprietor of the time, Tom Hodgson, who would lead the Town team out at Wembley four years later! I didn't understand why my Grandfather had stopped going to matches. He said it was the big crowds, which he feared would cram into Kenilworth Road. But, Grandad had seen the Town play in the Southern League in the early part of the 20th Century. So there may have been similar feelings to mine when Luton won the League Cup in 1988: "It ain't gonna get any better than this, so it might be an idea to make this my last Town match!"

My Grandfather was a promising footballer, but a a shrapnel wound in the First World War meant that he'd never be as good again. While even football was sometimes grim in terms of injuries sustained by players in the first half of the 20th Century. Grandad actually saw a Town player die on the pitch. So, tragedies like that put the Town's relegation fight into perspective.

A week later a whopping 23,096 turned up to see Luton draw 1-1 with fellow strugglers Chelsea, and from now until the end of the season gates were, in the main, good at Kenilworth Road. A narrow defeat at Burnley and a 1-1 draw at Sheffield United saw Luton fall back from 21st to 22nd (bottom place). But a Ron Futcher goal helped Luton beat Newcastle 1-0 at Kenilworth Road - I missed a family wedding to see Supermac's return, and smiled as the Newcastle fans responded to the "We hate Geordies!" chant with "We hate Cockneys!" Did they mean us?! Nearly 20,000 then saw Luton draw 0-0 at home to Stoke and Luton had climbed to third from bottom. A settled side of: Horn, John Ryan, Buckley, Anderson, Faulkner, Paul Futcher, Jimmy Ryan, Husband, Ron Futcher, West and

Aston seemed to be making a difference. Then, a 3-1 loss at title favourites Everton in front of 35,714 (the biggest crowd Luton played in front of all season) started a run of three defeats in a row (I blamed Alan West's new perm). A 2-1 defeat at QPR couldn't be condemned, but a 3-1 defeat at home to Coventry was poor.

Keith Barber returned in goal, and the next three fixtures were Carlisle away, and Leeds and Arsenal at home. Six points out of six would be unlikely... A win at Carlisle was expected, as the Cumbrians had looked out of their depth in Division One after their great start. Luton won 2-1.

"Welcome to the 'Super Leeds'" it said on my 10p programme. Fair enough. Leeds were the reigning League champions, and they had been the best team in England over the last half-a-dozen years. Some of the Yorkshire side's top stars, such as Billy Bremner, Allan Clarke and Peter Lorimer were absent at Kenilworth Road, but Johnny Giles, Norman Hunter, Paul Madeley, Paul Reaney and Eddie Gray were still around. Joe Jordan, Gordon McQueen and Duncan McKenzie were just making names for themselves, and Gabby Logan's dad Terry Yorath also played.

Leeds didn't look too super in the first quarter of an hour though, as goals from Peter Anderson and John Aston put Luton 2-0 ahead. Stunning stuff. Watching from the Oak Road End I saw Leeds fans amuse themselves by throwing lighted newspapers around in the Kenilworth Road End. Yes, who needed to watch *A Clockwork Orange*? A Joe Jordan goal made things tense, but Luton held on in front of a crowd of 23,048.

Leeds enjoyed something of a revival under
manager Jimmy Armfield, and they went on to
reach the European Cup final that season. Had they
not, the Town might have stayed up. More on why
later. Leeds hooligans stole the headlines in Paris, as
Leeds lost 2-0 to Bayern Munich. Leeds outplayed
the German side - Franz Beckenbauer, Gerd Muller,
Paul Breitner, Sepp Maier and all - but were on the
receiving end of some dubious decisions. Bayern
were also very fortunate to beat a Michel Platini-
inspired St. Etienne a year later at Hampden Park.
After the '75 final, Beckenbauer famously said,
because of the hooliganism by Leeds fans, that
English clubs should "just play on their own little
island." 10 years later English clubs were banned
from European football after the horrors of Heysel,
and Luton were one of the clubs who suffered as a
consequence.

Next up for the Town were the misfiring Gunners.
Half the Double side of '71 still remained, and they
had Alan Ball and a young Liam Brady too. So why
they had been so poor this season was a mystery.
Luton strolled to a 2-0 win in front of 22,300, with
goals from Jimmy Ryan and Ron Futcher. Strangely,
Luton's gates at home to Chelsea and Arsenal had
been bigger than when the Hatters had played at
Stamford Bridge and Highbury. But then Chelsea
and Arsenal were struggling, so maybe Luton had
more loyal supporters!

At the Arsenal game, a charming nine-year-old
Gunners fan challenged me to a fight on the
Kenilworth Road terrace. I was 15, so it was no

contest. WHALLOP! I went down. No, it would have been unwise to have hit a small kid in front of the Arsenal hordes behind me. The brat had nicked a scarf from another Town fan about my age, so I intervened. The lad was too timid to do anything. I can imagine where that nine-year-old ended up...

My maternal Grandmother, who was now living with us, would ask me when I came back from games: "Were there any ructions?" I think that she was secretly disappointed when I told her there hadn't been!

Disappointingly, nay, desperately disappointingly, three wins in a row had still left Luton in 21st place. Then things really fell apart over Easter (as they had in '70-'71). Ten goals conceded in two away games - 5-0 at soon-to-be champions Derby and 5-2 at Wolves - was something most Town fans probably didn't see coming. Derby's Roger Davies, a beanpole striker in the Peter Crouch mould (though a few inches shorter), helped himself to five goals at the Baseball Ground. Next, a 2-1 defeat at relegation rivals Spurs then seemed to have sealed the Town's fate. Back to the bottom we went, as Carlisle started to, unexpectedly, pick up points.

An unlikely win at home to Everton, however, lifted spirits. Peter Anderson scored both goals, and there must have been a temptation to play him up front more often. Bob Latchford scored for the Merseysiders, and after leaving Birmingham he had become one of the best number 9s in the country. Now, Luton have always befuddled their fans, and a 3-0 home win against Leicester and a 4-1 win at Birmingham meant an incredible sequence in the

Hatters last 12 games. Three defeats in a row, then three wins in a row, then three defeats in a row, and now three wins in a row!

The Leicester game was famous for Keith Weller's own goal. If there's ever been a better executed own goal, then I've never seen it. Keith casually sent a back pass past a scrambling Mark Wallington from the byline some 30 yards away. "It's a funny old game" as Jimmy Greaves would say. He must have seen Keith Weller's performances and Leicester's in their last two games at Kenilworth Road. Goal of the season hero to a zero for Keith in a year. The Foxes 4-0 win in the Cup had been well and truly avenged. Over 18,000 saw the fun, and Town fans couldn't contain their mockery at Weller's expense. Adrian Alston (back in place of Ron Futcher) and Jimmy Husband scored the other goals. Steve Litt was also in defence (in place of Paul Futcher).

Alston (two), Husband and John Ryan scored in the hammering of Brum. A most unexpected scoreline despite the Brummies disappointing season.

So, it came down to the last game of the season. Luton were third from bottom, with Spurs one place above, but being on the same number of points as the Hatters - 32. Spurs had a game in hand and were ahead of the Town on goal average (goal difference replaced goal average in 1976-77). On the last Saturday Luton were at home to Manchester City, while Spurs were at Arsenal, so Spurs would receive no favours there then. Indeed they didn't and lost. Carlisle were already down and Chelsea soon followed suit.

Manchester City had had a below par season. They had the best home form in the division along with Ipswich, but 12 away defeats had cost them any chance of winning the League. City also had an array of classy players in Colin Bell, Rodney Marsh, Dennis Tueart and Asa Hartford, and one of the country's best 'keepers in Joe Corrigan.

Before the game I was told on the Oak Road terrace that one of my best schoolfriends, Doug Robins, had died of leukaemia. It wasn't unexpected, but you can never be fully prepared for such bad news - not when you're 15, and your mate has died at the same age. This was to be another game I'd watch in a daze.

A Jimmy Ryan goal earnt Luton a point, and this meant for the first time since October that Luton were out of the bottom three. I walked onto the pitch at the end (it was okay to do that then at the end of the season), and a guy was telling me to kick a scared looking City fan who had been felled. I pretended to, but just gave the City fan the nod to scarper, as someone else might not be so humane.

So, Spurs had to beat Leeds in the last game of the season at White Hart Lane to stay up - and send the Hatters down. Leeds, though, had the European Cup final on their minds and played a weakened team. Normally you would have expected Leeds to get a draw at the very least at Spurs. Not this time. Spurs won 4-2. The following day I attended Doug's funeral. Yes, we were relegated, but football was only a game after all.

1975-76 - On the Brink

The 1974-75 season had been grim. Leading up to that season I'd lost my pet rabbit Candy (I still can't watch *Watership Down* without blubbing at the end), and that set the tone for what was to come personally and on the pitch. But, towards the end of the 1974-75 season, I did lose myself in Luton Central Library, researching Luton matches right back to their first season of League football back in 1897-98. I planned recording every result in the Hatters history. A bold undertaking for a 15-year-old, and I bailed out at the 1899-1900 season. Roger Wash was to have greater stamina...

1975 was certainly an eventful year. We moved to Warden Hill Road, I really started getting into music that year, it was my last year at school (I wasn't there much, as my rebellious nature had started to kick in), and my first sexual experience was not as embarrassing as trying to cover up several love bites on my neck. Despite relegation, Luton hung onto all their first team regulars, and Andy King was given his chance early in the season, after being a substitute for a few games in 1974-75 (as had been Lil Fuccillo). While Steve Litt started in the no. 6 shirt and not Paul Futcher. King scored on his full debut, as Luton beat Hull 2-0 at Kenilworth Road, with another youngster, Ron Futcher, scoring the other goal.

A young Sandor Simon was also making a name for himself for the Town in the Mid-Week League. He scored all three in a 3-0 win at home to Northampton. Sandor also went to Icknield High, and I remember a gang of us trying to tackle him as he dribbled past us with a tennis ball. He beat us on his own something like 15-1 in the school playground - or at least it seemed like it! That made me realise just how good even players at youth level were when they were on the books of a pro club. After Sandor left school I kept a keen eye on his career, but his career didn't take off for whatever reason. The boy was certainly gifted.

Luton's first away game of the 1975-76 season was against West Brom at the Hawthorns. As I'd had happy memories of Luton playing West Brom away, I thought why not pay a return visit. My main memory was of Ron Futcher thoroughly analyzing the pitch before the game, so it couldn't have been a classic. Luton lost 1-0.

Ronnie scored in the next game - a convincing 3-0 win over Chelsea at Kenilworth Road in front of 19,024 fans. Peter Anderson also scored and left-back Steve Buckley scored his first goal for the

Hatters - from the penalty spot. Steve was the closest you'd get, buildwise, to Fred Flintstone on a football pitch!

The Hatter Luton Town FC newspaper first appeared at the start of the 1975-76 season, and at just 10p was great value - more so than the titchy match programme, which was the same price. Only a mug would have bought both. Hands up...

A 2-0 win at Ian St John's Portsmouth had George Graham, then playing for Pompey, say the Town had "taught us a football lesson (*The Hatter*, Issue No. 3)". Andy King scored again, and Adrian Alston scored what turned out to be his last goal for Luton.

A dismal run then followed, after a 2-1 League Cup defeat at Darlington - and the Town's next win didn't come until October 18th, and a 1-0 win at home to Fulham. A rare Brian Chambers goal secured Luton's first victory in 8 games. The Hatters then failed to score in their next three games, though two 0-0 draws - at Forest and at home to Bristol City were respectable enough. Off the pitch, however, Luton were in trouble. Big trouble financially.

Three successive defeats came after a 4-0 hammering of York at Kenilworth Road. That victory was illuminated by a rare Alan West goal. A 1-0 home win over Orient in late November, and a 5-1 win at Charlton, with a brace each by Peter Anderson and Jimmy Husband, then lifted spirits. Then came a hammer blow - Peter Anderson was sold to Belgian side Royal Antwerp to keep the Town alive as a football club. Anderson was put in a horrible position. He either signed, or Luton probably folded. So, Anderson signed. What else could he do?

In amongst all the financial mayhem Alan Slough returned to Kenilworth Road for his testimonial. Alan had been in the Town first team when they were trying to avoid re-election in the '60s, and then he helped the club to two promotions. His appearance in the '75 FA Cup final with Fulham was something no Town fan would have begrudged him, though it seemed surreal to see him alongside Bobby Moore and Alan Mullery in the Fulham side. Luton beat Alan Slough All Stars 4-2, and Malcolm MacDonald made a formidable attacking duo with Frank Worthington, with Bruce Rioch and Chris Nicholl also in the All Stars team with the likes of Bob Wilson, Colin Todd, Brian Talbot and Howard Kendall. Alan Slough seemed a nice fella, and I remember he gave some of us coaching tips when he came to Warden Hill Junior School in the 1970-71 season.

Incredibly, despite the turmoil at the club, the Town were to go on a run of 8 victories in a row, beginning with the Orient win. Andy King scored in four successive games, while though he didn't score in the Town's 2-0 3rd Round FA Cup win at home to Blackburn, King scored in the 3-1 win at home to Portsmouth. That made it a goal for the teenager in five successive League games. Andy's sequence began with a goal in a 2-1 home win over Johnny Giles' West Brom, thus avenging that early season defeat.

Luton's winning run came to an abrupt end, with a

2-0 defeat at Norwich in the FA Cup, followed by a 3-0 loss at Bolton. While a 1-1 draw at Kenilworth Road in January between the Town and Forest was dreadful fare. I remember digging my hands deep into my jean jacket pockets at the Oak Road End, freezing cold, and bored out of my brains. Luton were going nowhere on this evidence, and, as for Forest, you couldn't see them back in the top flight any time soon - even with Brian Clough as manager, as he was for this game. The next season Forest won promotion and from there, er, did quite well...

Just 3,507 saw Luton win 3-2 at York and Luton were surprisingly still in contention for promotion. The York game was notable for being a game that Lil Fuccillo made his full debut in - and he scored. Luton's promotion hopes, though, were finally dashed by a run of spectacularly bad away performances - FOUR 3-0 defeats in succession. The Town's home form had still been good, however, with Sunderland (2-0), Southampton (1-0), and Carlisle (3-0) being defeated in succession at Kenilworth Road.

In March I had some fun with a Saints fan on the Kenilworth Road terrace, and I said to him, jokingly, "Who's the wanker in the no. 8 shirt?" It was Mick Channon. The Saints fan, a very likeable guy, endeared me to him further by being very confident about Southampton winning the FA Cup that season. I just scoffed at that. I hadn't learnt my Sunderland lesson obviously... Luton won 1-0 by the way, and Saints won by the same scoreline in the '76 Cup final against Manchester United.

The flat ending to the season was compounded by Andy King being sold to Everton for £35,000. Andy went on to become one of Everton's best loved players, and his chirpy character was well suited to Scouserville. Andy would also have won a stack of England caps in today's era I think. But, in the mid to late 1970s, Ray Wilkins, Glenn Hoddle, Bryan Robson and Graham Rix were coming through, and Trevor Brooking, Tony Currie, Terry McDermott, Ray Kennedy and Brian Talbot were established stars.

At least the Town finished the season well. Three successive wins, with three goals in each match, helped the Hatters to finish a respectable seventh. In the final game of the season, a 3-0 win at home to Blackpool, Ricky Hill made his full League debut for the Town. He'd made his first appearance as a substitute in the previous game, a 3-1 win at home to Bristol Rovers.

1976-77 - Fighting Back

There were really no high expectations for this season! No words of wisdom from Dusty, Nobby and Clank either, as *The Hatter* and the trio's Oak Road Enders Report had bitten the dust midway through '75-'76.

One bright spark at the start of the season was Ricky Hill, who scored in the Town's first two away games - a 3-1 defeat at Hull and a 2-1 win at Burnley. Dixie Deans had also scored in the latter, and the Hatters new number nine had opened his account with two goals against Sheffield United in the season opener. Luton won that game at Kenilworth Road 2-0, while Lil Fuccillo also started the season as a first team regular.

A 3-1 loss at Sunderland in the League Cup, a 1-1 draw at home to Forest, with Barry Butlin still in the promotion-bound Forest side, was followed by a crazy 4-3 defeat at the Valley against Charlton. Then it was Showbiz FC in town - Fulham.

Luton boy Alan Slough was now captain of a Fulham side that had George Best, Bobby Moore and Rodney Marsh in its line-up. Rodders scored one of the Fulham goals in front of nearly 20,000 fans as the visitors won 2-0.

A fine 2-1 win at Wolves after the Fulham game was then followed by a single goal defeat at Plymouth. Even in early October then Luton were annoyingly unpredictable, and, with a weak reserve side, there was little pressure on the first teamers.

In the home game against Hereford, the highlight was a rocket from Paul Futcher. It was Paul's first goal in League football, but John Gilbert Faulkner also dominated my memories of the day, as he unleashed a rocket of his own to his skilful central defensive partner, "Get rid of it, you f***er!" Paul Futcher wouldn't have lasted five minutes at Wimbledon in the 1980s (though the Dons, paradoxically, did have some talented creative players such as Dennis Wise)!

The 2-0 win over Hereford and a 1-1 draw at Carlisle signalled a mini revival, or so Hatters fans hoped. FA Cup holders Southampton soon put paid to that with a 4-1 victory at Kenilworth Road, with goal machine (at least at non-Division 1 level) Ted MacDougall scoring one of the Saints goals. Loyal Mick Channon, in his last season at Southampton, was also in the Saints side.

The Town's up and down form continued, with a 4-2 win at home to Bristol Rovers, and a 4-0 win at Notts County proving that Luton had a potency in front of goal. Jimmy Husband, Ron Futcher and

John Aston all went on to reach double figures goalswise for the season. At the back, though, the Hatters were liable to concede too many. A 4-2 loss at Millwall in mid-November being a case in point. I went to Brisbane Road to see another example of the Town's inconsistency, as we went down to a Laurie Cunningham-inspired Orient side by 1-0. That was on December 27th. I didn't realise what was to come a couple of days later - Luton 4 Chelsea 0. The Blues were going for promotion, and not many Town fans would have expected a win, let alone see the Londoners hammered. It was one of the Town's most notable performances of the whole decade.

I used to go to games at this time with a little gang - Gary Smith, Gerard Lannon and Gary Winn. There was, I remember, a particular gentleman in the Oak Road End, who Gary Winn and I were amused by. This guy wore a sheepskin coat, was built like Barney Rubble, and he applauded - with his fists... So, when Luton scored, it'd be knuckle on knuckle action. We hoped he never saw us laughing, because he may have been like Clint Eastwood's mule, and "didn't like people laffing, because he thinks they're laughing at him."

We also enjoyed a sex education lesson in the Maple Road section one time, as one bloke was telling his mate, in explicit detail, and at length, what sort of stuff him and his "lovely" girlfriend got up to. We learnt a lot, and our eyes (and ears) were on stalks. While, though not really sex-related, Gary Smith and I sniggered incessantly to an advertising board on the Bobbers Stand that promoted the wonders of 'W & L Erection'. Disappointingly, it was building-related.

New Year's Day saw Luton infuriate again - a 1-0 defeat at Bristol Rovers. Our gang then went to Halifax for a 3rd Round FA Cup tie. Luton won by a single goal, and I remember the endless back-to-back houses that seemed ideal for a Hovis ad. While it was the impressive Halifax Building Society HQ that dominated the skyline.

A week later and Town fans had the privilege of seeing football icon Billy Bremner do his nut. Luton were losing late in the game, and Bremner, Hull's captain, was unhappy when the Town equalised. Then he really flipped when Jimmy Husband converted a Lil Fuccillo cross in the 90th minute. Yes, Billy was a winner all right, but not on this occasion - and how the home crowd let him know about it.

A 3-0 win at Sheffield United followed, and Jimmy Husband, on a high from the Hull game, scored twice and set up the other for Ron Futcher. But, I don't remember the gang being over-confident, as we went up to Chester for the FA Cup 4th Round game.

With its Tudor buildings, Chester is a beautiful city. But it was a beast in a football sense in 1977. The cops there were on a par with the West Midlands, and one Town fan, who jokingly said that Hatters supporters were going to cause trouble, was summarily dragged by his hair round and round by a cop on his horse. With a ripple of his butt cheeks, and a sound like the crack of a rifle when fired, the horse farted in our direction. The cop, in now more benign mood, said wittily: "That's what he thinks of you." Yes, away fans in the '70s and '80s were universally seen as the scum of the earth. We all had a right to sing what Millwall fans appropriated: "No one likes us, but we don't care." As for the game itself, we didn't want a replay. Chester obliged, and won 1-0 thanks to a late goal. Not really what we had in mind...

Luton had, though, won their last two League games and then made it 9 League wins in a row. A 1-1 home draw with Plymouth ended the winning sequence. But two more wins made it 11 victories in 12 games, and just one point dropped up to early April, since the loss to Bristol Rovers on New Year's Day!

A 2-1 win at Forest and a win by the same scoreline at Fulham (Bestie didn't show, Rodney Marsh's last game in English football) - I remember a torturous trip to Craven Cottage, which took an age to reach by coach because of the London traffic - were two results that stood out. While Ron Futcher was inspired in a 2-0 home win at home to Charlton. Ronnie scored both goals, including a stunning solo effort. Ron Futcher, it has to be said, was a frustrating player to watch. He could look top class, but on other occasions he looked out of his depth. But, Ron was a bit of a character, and fun to watch, because you never knew which Ronnie would turn up.

Luton's gates had been disappointing, with no match attracting 15,000 until Wolves on March 5th. Luton were right in the hunt for promotion after 7 straight wins, and Wolves were riding high too.

19,200 saw goals by Husband and Fuccillo sink the star-studded Black Country boys. I was one of the 19,200, as was Gary Smith. At the Oak Road End, Gary was bored and entertained himself by burning holes in his Luton scarf with a cigarette - and I thought I had a short attention span!

The Town's 5-0 win at home to Carlisle on March 26th was a fantastic performance, and we even had an entertaining referee in Roger Kirkpatrick for the game. In truth it could have been double figures. Paul Futcher, of all people, had a go at penalty-taking and missed. His brother Ron had a goal disallowed, John Aston had one effort hit a post, and Jimmy Husband missed a sitter. Ronnie, Johnny and Jimmy did all score, though, as did Alan West and Lil Fuccillo.

A nice trip through the New Forest was then spoilt as I saw the Hatters actually lose a League game - 1-0 at Southampton. Not a great weekend, as I was worried about losing my job as well! Near the ground, we nearly didn't wake up a friend who was asleep as we prepared to get off the coach, while that Southampton defeat triggered a nightmare run of results, with the Easter curse striking again.

No wins in five, and four defeats, including a 2-0 loss at Chelsea in front of nearly 32,000, and a rare home defeat (2-1 to Millwall), was at least partly compensated by a 4-2 win at home to a promotion-chasing Notts County side. A young loan signing from Ipswich, David Geddis, scored and he looked an outstanding prospect, as did Ricky Hill who also scored, and Ron bagged two. Milija Aleksic was also now the Town's goalkeeper, and, because of his surname and agility, he was given the nickname 'Elastic' by the Oak Road End. When the gang saw Geddis and Aleksic in the Town car park there was a temptation to ask for autographs, but opportunity missed. The pair both went on to pick up FA Cup winners medals - Geddis with Ipswich in 1978, and Aleksic with Spurs in 1981.

One bitter comment I made amuses me after Orient shut up shop to get a goalless draw at Kenilworth Road in April. On the back of the programme I called Orient the "most boring side I've ever seen". Glenn Roeder, Derek Possee and future Hatter Tony Grealish were in the Os line-up. Another team that had been cynical I felt at Kenilworth Road were Blackburn Rovers. Losing 2-0 at Luton in early January, Blackburn players were struggling to keep their feet on an icy surface - or were keen to persuade the referee to take the teams off... The match was abandoned after 51 minutes. But, no matter, Luton won the replayed fixture 2-0!

A 4-2 defeat at Cardiff in April included a goal from Cardiff's Robin Friday. His goal was made famous, or, more pertinently, infamous thanks to a photograph of Friday giving Town 'keeper Milija Aleksic a V sign after he had scored - the two had been at loggerheads earlier in the game. The photograph decades later was used for a sleeve of a Super Furry Animals single. As for Robin Friday, his Wikipedia entry suggests that he was the king of football's bad boys. His life, probably unsurprisingly, was tragically short.

Luton finished the season in sixth position, and most of the side were going to be around for years -

if Luton could keep hold of them. Paul Price was at right-back, Steve Buckley at left-back, Brian Chambers, Hill, Fuccillo and Alan West were in midfield, and then there were the Futcher twins (who were still only 20). The future looked bright, the future looked, er, orange... Wolves (champions), Chelsea (runners-up), and Forest (third) also underlined the quality of the 2nd Division in 1976-77. Forest won the League a year later, with a few impressive additions, but the nucleus of the 1977-78 side could only finish three places higher than the Hatters a year earlier!

1977-78 - Pleat's Reign Begins Quietly...

Luton began the season with a formidable squad, and Harry Haslam added to it by signing forward Phil Boersma from Liverpool. Boersma had been a player Haslam had tried to sign for years, and he was in the team for Luton's pre-season friendly at home to Arsenal. In that game, Milija Aleksic saved a Malcolm MacDonald penalty, and goalkeeping legend Pat Jennings made his Gunners debut. Luton fans were also to see one of their favourites, John Aston, leave the club early in the season.

Steve Buckley was an unlikely source of goals for the Town early on in '77-'78, and he scored three in the first five games, including the only goal of the season opener at home to Orient. Luton then lost by a single goal at Oldham in their first League away fixture, but responded to that defeat with a magnificent 3-1 League Cup win at Wolves, with Phil Boersma scoring his first Hatters goal. A 7-1 annihilation of Charlton followed, and Jimmy

Husband filled his boots with four. Buckley scored again, and youngsters Ricky Hill and Gary Heale also netted. Another youngster, David Carr, had scored at Molineux after coming on as a sub, and Husband scored his first of the season against the Second Division champions. Buckley and Boersma then scored in a 2-1 win at Bristol Rovers, and the Town were flying with three wins in a row and 12 goals scored in the process. Blackburn, however, put a stop to the Town's free scoring as the Hatters fired blanks in the mid-September game at Kenilworth Road. Then next up were the not-so-mighty Tottenham Hotspur at White Hart Lane.

A humiliating exit from the First Division in bottom place meant that Spurs were smarting, and 32,700 watched as the home side scored two goals without reply against the Town. After a handful of games Spurs were already top, and they'd take some catching. A young midfielder called Glenn Hoddle looked a special talent - as he was to prove in the return fixture...

A 3-2 reverse at newly promoted Brighton was a more unexpected setback. Another big crowd, 25,132, saw Husband and Ron Futcher score for Luton. Then four successive victories (the Town tended to go regularly on winning or losing streaks in the '70s) put the Town in and around the promotion places, with a 4-1 win at Cardiff a standout result. Ricky Hill scored a goal in that game, and, in his next game, famously left George Best on his backside, as he waltzed past the fallen genius during a 1-0 home win over Fulham. That iconic photograph of Ricky heralded his arrival as a bona fide star in his own right.

The Fulham game was also one of those "I was there - or thought I was" games. My maternal Grandmother had died two days earlier, so football wasn't a priority at the time. I've got the programme, so I'll take that as proof that I was among the sub-13,000 that did watch.

Another run followed the Fulham victory - a dreadful one of 10 games without a win, including seven in the League. While three meritorious displays against the previous season's Division One runners-up, Manchester City, in the League Cup just reminded Hatters fans how frustrating Luton could be to watch. A 1-1 draw at home, with a Ron Futcher shot putting the Town ahead in front of 16,443, was followed by a goalless draw at Maine Road. The Town's Gary Heale then scored twice as the Hatters lost a second replay, which was at Maine Road, 3-2. A certain future Luton legend - Brian Stein, made his Town debut in that game. Both Paul and Ron Futcher would also eventually end up at City, and Paul missed the 3-2 game after being seriously injured in a car crash.

In the League Luton played well at Bolton, only to lose 2-1 to a Lancashire side that topped the table in early November, and who were keen to make up for just missing out on promotion two seasons running. A 1-1 draw at Sunderland was a fine result, but a 3-1 loss at Mansfield was a shocker. That inconsistency again. It may have been this game that my friends told me about, when a Hatters fan turned up on a bitterly cold day dressed in a T-shirt and shades, and said to all those keeping a distance from him: "This is what the Army does for you."

The disappointing run came to an end on December 10th in unlikely fashion - a 1-0 win at Southampton, who ended up promoted. Ron Futcher scored the winner. Notable at this time were the size of the crowds the Town were playing in front of. They'd dipped below 7,000 at home for some games, while, at away games in the League during the autumn to early winter, Luton had played in front of 20,113 at Bolton, 26,915 at Sunderland and 19,909 at Southampton. The first League Cup replay at Maine Road had also attracted 28,254. This was in addition to the 25,000 plus crowds at Tottenham and Brighton earlier in the season.

A 1-1 draw with lowly Mansfield at Kenilworth Road came immediately after the win at The Dell, and then another of Luton's eccentric performances saw them earn a 3-3 draw at Crystal Palace on Boxing Day in front of another sizeable crowd - 22,027. Brian Stein also made his full League debut at Selhurst Park against Palace.

At least the Town were ending the year well, and a 4-0 home thumping of Sheffield United a day after the Palace game saw Brian Stein, a signing from Edgware Town, grab his first goals in a Luton shirt. Stein scored twice in the no. 7 shirt, while, curiously, Ricky Hill wore the no. 8 shirt. The number 7 shirt was to become Ricky Hill's, as he rose to become one of the most skilful midfield players in England, and the number 8 shirt was to become very much associated with Brian Stein. Stein looked a very promising acquisition, though, in his early days at Luton, he was rather head down and heavily reliant on his pace. But the awareness that was to make him one of the country's most feared strikers was to come later. The win over Sheffield United was backed up by a 1-0 win over Brighton, again at home, on the last day of 1977, with Phil Boersma scoring the winner. A decent crowd, too, of over 13,000.

A 0-0 draw at Orient early in 1978 was the precursor to three games in a row against Oldham Athletic. Luton drew an FA Cup 3rd Round tie 1-1 with the Lancashire club at Kenilworth Road, but the Town won the replay 2-1 thanks to two Boersma goals. Oldham got their revenge, however, with a 1-0 League win at Kenilworth Road. It was the Town's first defeat in 9 games.

The first few weeks of '78 were turbulent. Steve Buckley was sold to Derby, and, after much speculation, Harry Haslam departed to become manager of Sheffield United. A lot of us were initially underwhelmed by Harry's replacement - David Pleat. Pleat was the first team coach, and, being in his early 30s, was just too inexperienced it seemed. But, in my opinion, David Pleat turned out to be Luton's greatest manager - and we've had few duds.

David Pleat took over with the team showing its Jekyll and Hyde form again. A goalless draw at Charlton, with Paul Futcher's return a welcome highlight, was followed by a 4-0 mauling by Millwall in the FA Cup 4th Round (Pleat's first game in charge). Less than 6,000 turned up for a 1-1 home draw with Bristol Rovers in early February, and Pleaty's first programme notes, before that game, were humble: "I must tackle the future and hope that no one will be disappointed." He also stated his footballing philosophy: "I want to win and win with style." We would also lose with style, too, circa the 1982-83 season, before DP's memorable season finale at Manchester City.

Before the Millwall and Bristol Rovers games Luton had entertained an Italian Under 21 side that included Fulvio Collovati and Antonio Cabrini. Ronnie scored in a 1-1 draw.

Utility players such as David Carr and Graham Jones were by now playing regularly. Carr having worn four different shirt numbers and Jones five by mid-March!

A 2-0 defeat at Blackburn in mid-February was mostly remembered for the treacherous nature of the pitch. Lil Fuccillo was stretchered off at Ewood Park, after he'd landed on his head following a collision. What was it with Luton-Blackburn games and frozen pitches!

Tottenham were next up, and our gang came in with some fans who seemed cheerful enough as we went in the Oak Road End. Then, when we were surrounded by them, out came their Spurs scarves. Uh-oh. Luckily, they saw us as kids, so didn't batter us. Spurs certainly did, winning 4-1, with two of their goals coming from Glenn Hoddle, as he put in a masterclass performance in front of the Town's biggest home crowd of the season - 17,024.

Luton's season then petered out, and home gates were really poor for most of the time. Only 6,029 turned up to see the Hatters beat Cardiff 3-1 in early March. This was followed by a 1-0 defeat to

Fulham.

The Hatters won their next three home games, which included a 4-0 thrashing of Blackpool and a 2-1 win over Bolton, the eventual champions, as, amazingly, Spurs only sneaked a promotion place when finishing third - above Brighton & Hove Albion on goal difference. Between those three home games, the Town had also been whalloped 4-1 away to Sheffield United.

With no win in the last six games of the season, and with the last three games ending in defeat, a massive overhaul of the squad was looking necessary. Thankfully I missed the last home game of the season on April 22nd, because I was watching Barton Rovers in the FA Vase final at Wembley with my Dad and some family friends. It seemed like a lot of Town fans had come to support Bedfordshire's first team at Wembley since the Hatters in 1959. Luton lost 2-1 to Division Two runners-up Southampton, and Rovers lost 2-1 to Newcastle Blue Star. It was strange to hear the Luton score come through and feel slightly detached. Luton finished the season in a not-so-lucky 13th place.

1978-79 - Still "Second Division Rubbish"

With new signing from Peterborough Chris Turner the Town's new captain and centre-half, the start of the season saw a team that was very much David Pleat's. The experienced striker Bob Hatton came from Blackpool, and he seemed a good foil for the promising Brian Stein. While goalscoring winger David Moss, a record £110,000 signing from Swindon, could make up for the loss of John Aston the previous season. Mal Donaghy, who had been signed from Larne in Northern Ireland, was an unknown quantity, but he went straight into the team, as did Kirk Stephens, a full-back from non-League Nuneaton, where Pleat had been manager. Youngster Mark Aizlewood was also a regular early in 1978-79. On the downside, the Futcher twins had been sold to Manchester City. Paul being sold for £350,000 - then a British record transfer fee for a defender. Stalwarts John Faulkner and Jimmy Husband also left the club. Extraordinarily, only Lil Fuccillo and Milija Aleksic were in the starting line-up for the first game of '77-'78 and '78-'79. The massive overhaul had happened...

The Pleat Revolution began in scintillating fashion - a 6-1 thrashing of Oldham at Kenilworth Road. New boys Hatton and Moss made an immediate impact with two goals apiece, Stein also scored, and Lil Fuccillo scored from the spot, which he also did in the Town's next game - a 3-1 defeat at Crystal Palace. Over 24,000 then saw relegated Newcastle overcome the Hatters 1-0 at St. James' Park.

A 2-0 League Cup win at home to Wigan, thanks to two Stein goals, was followed by a 3-0 win at Kenilworth Road against Charlton, with Ricky Hill, Stein and Hatton all on target. Though looking strong at home the Town had lost their first three away games, after they went down 2-0 at Bristol Rovers. Another big home win, 7-1 against Cardiff, saw Stein and Moss score twice, and Hatton netted again. Fuccillo also scored his third penalty of the season as the Hatters made it four home wins out of four. Cambridge then ended that run in a 1-1 draw at Kenilworth Road, though Stein made it 7 goals in 8 games for him in the season. At least the crowd was nearly 11,000 for the fairly local clash, as gates were still generally poor for Hatters home games.

Frustrated with Luton's away performances, Pleat was leaving out the likes of Alan West, Graham Jones, Hill and Fuccillo. Donaghy was shifted to the centre of defence from midfield for the trip to Sheffield United in late September, and that move brought immediate reward with a 1-1 draw - Bob Hatton the scorer.

In early October, Luton moved into the 4th Round of the League Cup with a 2-1 home win over Crewe, and then goals from Fuccillo and Stein were enough to see off Wrexham 2-1 at Kenilworth Road in the League. A clean sheet at Blackburn ensured a point, and then came Luton's third big win of the season at Kenilworth Road. Notts County were put to the sword 6-0, with the new forward line of Stein (2), Hatton and Moss (a goal apiece) firing again. Alan West and Fuccillo also scored. So, Hatters fans had been treated to 25 goals by the Town in their first six League games at home, with only four conceded.

Two defeats in a row - 3-2 at Orient and 1-0 at home to Leicester - took the wind out of Luton's sails after 7 games unbeaten. But Luton then did what they often do, surprise us. Villa Park in the 4th Round of the League Cup was the scene.

On November 8th, Luton played 1st Division Aston Villa with no away win yet that season. The strikeforce of Hatton and Stein, though, scored the goals in a superb 2-0 win in front of 32,727. Hill and Donaghy were in the team alongside Stein, and this was the game that established that trio as the cornerstone of the Luton side for the next decade, which culminated in that even bigger League Cup moment just under 10 years later at Wembley.

Not all Town fans were happy though. A brother of a friend of mine went in among the Villa fans to start a fight, but there seemed few takers! The hardcore of the Oak Road End, the fellas behind the goal and high up the terracing were, in the '70s, mostly made up of fans from the Lewsey Farm and

Farley Hill areas of Luton, and they'd both chant the name of their area just to underline the fact. Strangely, a chant fight of "Celtic!" "Rangers!" would also ring out on occasion. So, some Scottish and Irish ancestry there! I remember being on the outer fringes of the centre of the Luton Town universe occasionally, and let's just say I know how the sardines feel. I felt I was almost suffocating there during a big game against Orient once, so I had to use physical force to set myself free! Only the bravest could stay there long. The guy who was looking for trouble at Villa Park, however, came from Limbury, so being a hardcore Oak Road Ender was not an exclusive club...

Luton's disappointing away form in the League continued with a 2-0 defeat at Oldham, and David Pleat was strengthening his goalkeeping options by bringing in David Lawson from Everton and Jake Findlay from Aston Villa. Lawson came in briefly for three games, beginning with the 2-0 win at Kenilworth Road against Newcastle. Brian Stein netted his 12th goal of the season against the Geordies, and Chris Turner scored his first goal in a Hatters shirt. A first away win in the League then came at Charlton, with Hatton and Moss scoring in a 2-1 victory. But the few weeks before Christmas were dismal, and Lawson's third game for the Town came in a 3-0 loss at home to Sunderland. In Chris Turner's absence the three Sunderland goals came from headers, when players were left unmarked. I wrote angrily after the game: "Luton just didn't compete." It didn't get much better in the next home game, when Jake Findlay made his Hatters debut (Paul Price also scored!). Luton went down 2-1 to Preston.

A quarter-final League Cup tie at Leeds was a game I wasn't too concerned about, as I'd had a dream you see. In that dream (the night before the Leeds game) Luton had been 2-0 down, but had come back to win. I went to the game with a hacking cough, and we got off the coach in a muddy car park and were escorted by grumpy police. When Luton were losing 3-0 my gang reminded me of my dream, and Leeds fans chanted "Second Division rubbish" at us. Nice. The dream never came true either... While coming out out of the ground, half a brick came sailing out over a stand towards us Luton fans. I heard a yelp, and a friend I hadn't seen for a while had been struck by said missile in his back! A few familiar faces were in and around Elland Road, but we all had more "Second Division rubbish" to look forward to after the 4-1 defeat.

On the coach home I had an interesting chat with a guy I'd never met before, and have never seen since. He was raving about Public Image Limited (Google them children, and John Lydon, Keith Levene and Jah Wobble), and on the back of his enthusiasm I bought their debut LP, though I'd loved their first single. Anyway, the time flew by before I got off the coach into the cold December night in Luton, with the hacking cough now in overdrive. Three days later the Town lost 3-1 at Brighton, with Godfrey Ingram making a rare start in place of Brian Stein, who'd scored in the loss to Leeds.

A Boxing Day win at home to Millwall (2-0) ended a run of four successive defeats. Mossy scoring both goals. Only 6,068 turned up, as the Winter of Discontent was kicking in, and three of Luton's games were postponed, due to the weather, from early December to the New Year's Day fixture at home to Stoke. Luton ended the year losing 1-0 at Fulham, and they began 1979 with an FA Cup defeat at York, going down 2-0. 28,177 fans had seen the Town's cup tie at Leeds, but only 6,730 saw the Town's inglorious FA Cup exit at Bootham Crescent.

Brian Stein was on the bench for Luton's home game against Bristol Rovers, and striker Steve Taylor, signed from Oldham, made his debut. Just 6,002 saw the Hatters 3-2 victory, and the Greek god that was Paul Price scored again, with Ricky Hill and David Moss (his 10th of the season) getting the other goals.

David Lawson returned in goal for a nil-nil draw at Cambridge in February, but the previously injured Jake Findlay returned the next week for the 1-1 draw with Sheffield United at Kenilworth Road. As for Milija Aleksic, he'd been recently sold to Tottenham. Two unlikely goalscorers, Chris Turner and Alan West, then helped the Town to a 2-1 home win against Blackburn a fortnight later. Barry Silkman, a gifted player, made his Town debut in that game after signing from Palace on loan.

Easily the Town's biggest crowd of the season - 14,205 - turned up to see West Ham give us a 4-1 beating, though the scoreline flattered the Hammers. Steve Taylor, at least, headed in his first Luton goal past Phil Parkes. While, at Notts County, Bob Hatton ended a barren run of not scoring. But with Hill, Stein, Moss and Fuccillo all out of the Town's starting line-up, the Hatters succumbed to a 3-1 defeat in early March.

Wayne Turner was to make his Town debut by the end of the season, as was one of football's biggest characters - Alan Birchenall. But, again Luton had had a disappointing season, and they finished 5th from bottom, with just two points more than relegated Sheffield United. Two wins in the last 13 games of the season did not augur well for 1979-80 either. Two home wins, 4-1 against Burnley and 2-0 against Fulham, were all Luton fans could enjoy between the 2-1 home win against Orient on the 10th of March to the 2-0 defeat at Wrexham in the last game of the season nearly two months later. At least Luton supporters had the satisfaction of seeing the two biggest home wins in the Division that season. But the Town should have been at the other end of the table, such was the strength of their squad.

1979-80 - Good Times Round the Corner

In the close season, Luton splashed out a club record £200,000 to sign centre-half Mike Saxby from Mansfield, and he replaced Chris Turner as the Town's first choice centre-half. Steve Taylor moved in the opposite direction in a £75,000 deal with Mansfield. While highly-rated midfielder Tony Grealish, a signing from Orient, was also expected to be a great buy for the Town.

The season didn't start well... A 3-0 League Cup loss at Gillingham in the revamped League Cup (now two legs for the early stages) was followed by a 1-1 draw at home - and a 4-1 defeat on aggregate. But at least Mark Aizlewood scored his first goal in a Luton shirt. However, Aizlewood and Saxby were both missing from the Town's first League game of the season - a 1-1 draw at home to Cambridge.

Wayne Turner replaced Aizlewood, and Alan Birchenall replaced Saxby at centre-half! Saxby returned for the 3-2 defeat at Bristol Rovers, with David Moss getting both goals to make it three goals in two games. Ricky Hill and Bob Hatton then netted in the Hatters first victory of the season - 2-1 over Orient at home. But it was in the month of September that the Town were to give notice that they were serious promotion contenders.

David Moss and Ricky Hill had scored 10 goals between them by mid-September, and Moss scored two and Hill one in a 3-1 win at Leicester on

September 1st. Over 10,000 were then at Luton's home game with Swansea City, which resulted in a 5-0 triumph for the Town. Moss scored twice again, Hill scored again (scoring for the third game in a row), and Hatton and Alan West completed the Swans misery. Two goalless draws - away at Notts County and at home to Oldham - were also a sign that Luton were tight defensively this season, with Mal Donaghy now at left-back, after starting the season in midfield (Mal was a player who made football look easy, and Alex Ferguson later likened him to a Rolls-Royce).

Hill, Hatton and Moss then all scored yet again as Fulham were beaten 3-1 at Craven Cottage. A rare loss came at Cardiff in early October (2-1, Hatton the scorer), before a Hatton hat-trick helped Luton beat Bristol Rovers 3-0 at Kenilworth Road. Notable results followed, too, a 2-0 home win against Sunderland (Moss 2 - 10 goals in 11 League games), watched by 13,504, and a 2-1 win at West Ham (Stein and Saxby both scoring) in front of 25,049. A slight hiccup was the 1-1 home draw with Preston, but a 2-1 victory at Cambridge made it four wins in five. Mossy scored in both games, with Hatton also scoring at Cambridge's Abbey Stadium. While it was a relief to see Brian Stein score at Upton Park, as it was his first goal in 14 matches that season. Mike Saxby also scored his first Hatters goal during the win over West Ham.

A big crowd of 19,619 then watched Luton's home match with QPR. Saxby scored again in a 1-1 draw with our West London promotion rivals. Yes, Luton were riding high for the first time in a long time.

A 0-0 draw at Burnley stretched Luton's unbeaten run to 7, until the run ended with a 3-2 home defeat to Birmingham in late November. A 2-1 win at Shrewsbury, with goals from Stein and Hatton, was then followed by a 1-1 draw at Kenilworth Road against Newcastle. Home gates were also certainly picking up now, and 13,720 watched the Birmingham game, with 14,845 at the Newcastle match. Moss scored in both home games, and in mid-December he'd scored 14 League goals for the season so far - a staggering total for a winger. Hatton reached double figures for the season, too, with a goal at Wrexham, but it came in a 3-1 defeat. Along with Moss and Hatton's regular strikes, Brian Stein was finding his goal touch on a regular basis at last, and he scored two in the 3-0 home win over Charlton, with Hatton collecting his 11th goal of the campaign in that match. Luton's last game of the '70s was, rather appropriately, at Orient - a club they'd been promoted alongside in 1970. Mossy scored two in a 2-2 draw.

Just before the Orient game the Luton-Watford rivalry had been renewed on Boxing Day. 20,227 were at Vicarage Road to see Kirk Stephens head the only goal of the game - his first goal for the Town too! Luton were now second in the table - a point behind Chelsea, and ahead of Newcastle on goal difference (Luton had the joint best goal difference in the division at this point).

It was to be Chelsea that Luton would host on New Year's Day. I actually began the '80s falling down the stairs at my home in Warden Hill Road (and I wasn't even drunk, honest, guv), and I thought this was a bad omen for the decade to come. I was wrong, re the Town's fortunes at least.

I wrote that the Luton-Chelsea game was: "The most thrilling game I've yet witnessed." It was a 3-3 draw, three goals were disallowed, and a penalty was initially given then the decision was reversed. The surface, I wrote, was "tricky", but it certainly helped the game as a spectacle. There was some crowd trouble too, among the 19,717, and a teenage lad with a skinhead haircut was bawling his eyes out as we spilled over onto the pitch from the Oak Road End. Just a case of having to. I felt strangely calm, as hooliganism just seemed normal then. After the game a Chelsea thug told me to give him my woollen scarf. I said "No", muttered "Prat" at him, and walked off hoping he wasn't too determined to get his 'trophy'. That scarf's destiny was fixed, and I proudly wore it at the League Cup final against Arsenal at Wembley in 1988. It's also on the front cover of this book.

By the way, Mal Donaghy, a star of that '88 side, scored his first League goal in that epic Chelsea game. Saxby and Moss (of course) also scored. The 3-3 thriller really was a taster for what would become the most glorious decade in Luton Town FC's history. But I'll let someone else write that story...

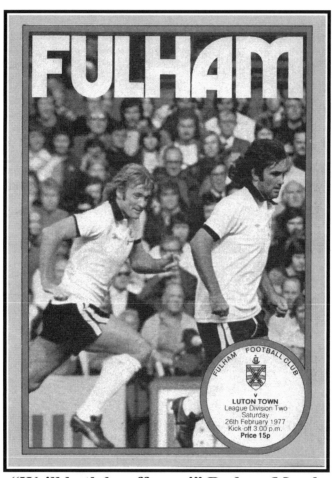

"We'll both be off soon!" Rodney Marsh and George Best on the cover of the Fulham v Luton progamme, 1976-77.

Cover of Leeds v Luton 1978-79 League Cup programme

References

Personal Knowledge
Luton Town FC programmes and year books
Wikipedia
Luton Town Football Club - The Full Record; Roger
Wash & Simon Pitts

Internal photographs by Paul Rance

About the Author

Paul Rance co-founded Peace & Freedom Press in 1985, and launched the booksmusicfilmstv.com website in 2005. He is a member of The Peace & Freedom Band, who were one of the first British rock groups to release music in the MP3 format. Born in Luton, Bedfordshire in 1959, Paul now lives in Lincolnshire.

Available from the same author in paperback and Kindle format.

Luton Town F.C.'s 50 Greatest Players
The obvious names are there - Syd Owen, Joe Payne, Malcolm MacDonald, Ricky Hill. But, there's also names that may have been forgotten.

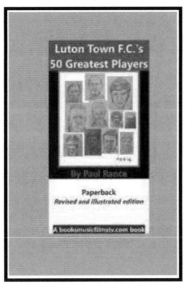

English football's first alien superstar - Luton's Luke Knoblitz
Luton's alien soccer star who rewrote the record books...

Luke Knoblitz was English and British football's first alien superstar. In the 2040s, Luke lands on a Luton hill and ends up as the greatest player in Luton City's history.

As well as stardom at Luton, Luke had an illustrious international career with England. When becoming tired of football, Luke Knoblitz then went on to become a successful cricketer for Bedfordshire and England. He also dabbled in music and made a very successful album with singing legend Tom O'Hawk.

Luke liked the girls, and his meeting with Leeds female hooligan gang the White Rose Bunny Boilers became a scandal that rocked football in the 2040s. Luke was also beaten up by Irish twins, who he had cheated on.

Meet the other great characters of mid-late 21st Century English football in *Luke Knoblitz - English Football's First Alien Superstar*. Be amazed by Jimmy Suitcase's and Jan Zsyzsziszowsky's behaviour, flinch at the antics of fearsome manager Alison Curvaceous, cringe at the team talks of cliche manager Jason Shattlodes, and suspend your belief reading about the exploits of almost unbeatable Chelsea 'keeper Billy Bubblehands.

50 Great Moments and Memories of the 1960s
From a British perspective, here's a look back at some of the greatest moments and people from the 1960s, including The Beatles, First Man on the Moon, Woodstock, Bob Dylan, Muhammad Ali, Twiggy, David Bailey, England winning the World Cup, The Rolling Stones, Martin Luther King, James Bond, *Doctor Who* and *Star Trek*.

Made in Luton

Photo by Peter Rance

More info on paulrance.com

INDEX

Bristol City 17, 24, 29, 33, 41, 45, 48, 50, 71
Bristol Rovers 59, 74, 76, 78, 79, 84, 87, 88, 91, 95, 97, 98
Brooking, Trevor 30, 58, 74
Buckley, Steve 60, 63, 70, 71, 82, 83, 84, 87
Burnden Park 43
Burnley 15, 28, 32, 48, 61, 63, 75, 96, 99
Burridge, John 40
Busby, Viv 19, 32, 37, 39, 40
Butlin, Barry 41, 44, 48, 50, 52, 53, 55, 57, 58, 59, 75
Cabrini, Antonio 88
Cambridge United 91, 95, 97, 98
Campbell, Alan 39
Candy 69
Cardiff City 24, 38, 43, 49, 81, 84, 88, 91
Cardinal Newman School 38
Carlisle United 20, 23, 41, 47, 50, 54, 59, 60, 64, 66, 67, 73, 76, 80
Carr, David 84, 88
Carrick, Willie 40
Celtic 93
Chambers, Brian 60, 71, 82
Channon, Mick 73, 76
Charlton Athletic 22, 28, 29, 71, 75, 79, 83, 84, 87, 91, 93, 99
Charlton, Bobby 22, 27
Charlton, Jack 49
Chelsea 56, 60, 61, 63, 65, 67, 70, 77, 80, 82, 99, 100
Chester FC 61, 78, 79
Chester Avenue 49
Chiles, Adrian 53
The City Ground 21
Clarke, Allan 64
Clemence, Ray 16, 25, 56, 57

Clough, Brian 58, 73
Collins, John 14
Collovati, Fulvio 88
Corrigan, Joe 68
Court, David 19, 34
Coventry City 22, 59, 64
Craven Cottage 79, 98
Crewe Alexandra 42, 92
Crouch, Peter 66
Cruyff, Johan 27
Cruse, Peter 48
Crystal Palace 28, 48, 51, 86, 91, 95
Cunningham, Laurie 77
Currie, Tony 20, 74
Cyprus National Team 18
Dad, Peter Rance 25, 29, 30, 38, 39, 43, 62, 89
The Damned United 58
Darlington FC 71
Davie, Sandy 14
Davies, Roger 66
Deans, Dixie 75
Del Boy 16
The Dell 86
Derby County 61, 66, 87
Donaghy, Mal 10, 11, 90, 91, 92, 98, 100
Dunstable Town 27
Dusty, Nobby and Clank 75
Dyson, Keith 33
Eastwood, Clint 77
Edgware Town 86
Eire National Team 18
Elland Road 94
England Ladies 30
England National Team 18, 20, 24, 37, 45, 74
European Cup 36
Everton 49, 64, 66, 74, 93

Ewood Park 88

FA Cup 20, 21, 29, 30, 37, 41, 42, 43, 44, 50, 51, 55, 56, 62, 72, 73, 76, 78, 79, 81, 87, 95

Farley Hill 93

The Fast Show 34

FA Vase final 89

Faulkner, John 35, 36, 37, 38, 55, 57, 60, 63, 76, 90

Ferguson, Alex 98

Fern, Rodney 24, 36, 37, 38, 39, 40, 41, 48, 60

Filbert Street 60

Findlay, Jake 10, 93, 95

Finney, Tom 47, 48

First World War 63

Flintstone, Fred 71

Football Combination 48

Francis, Gerry 35, 45

Francis, Trevor 23, 24, 40, 60

French, Graham 14, 41, 42

Fretwell, David 50

Friday, Robin 81

Fuccillo, Lil 70, 73, 75, 78, 80, 82, 88, 90, 91, 92, 95

Fulham 19, 27, 28, 31, 38, 45, 50, 71, 72, 75, 76, 79, 84, 85, 89, 95, 96, 98

Futcher, Paul 10, 11, 61, 62, 63, 67, 70, 76, 80, 82, 85, 87, 90

Futcher, Ron 61, 62, 63, 65, 67, 70, 76, 78, 79, 80, 82, 84, 85, 86, 88, 90

Game, Reg 58

Garner, Alan 32, 35, 37, 43, 48, 55, 57, 60

Geddis, David 80, 81

Gemmill, Archie 61

Giles, Johnny 58, 64, 72

Gillingham FC 97

Givens, Don 10, 11, 18, 30, 34, 35, 41, 45

Glover, Brian 22

Goodeve, Ken 38
Google 94
Graham, George 71
Gran (maternal) at Barton 42, 66, 85
Gran (paternal) at Luton 21
Grandad (maternal) 16, 42, 62, 63
Gray, Eddie 64
Grealish, Tony 81, 97
Greaves, Jimmy 23, 67
Green, Rodney 16, 25
Hales, Derek 38, 43
Halifax Building Society HQ 78
Halifax Town 78
Halom, Vic 27, 28, 32, 38, 39, 40, 44, 55
Hampden Park 65
Harford, Mick 20
Hartford, Asa 68
Haslam, Harry 10, 37, 38, 39, 61, 62, 83, 87
Haslam, Keith 37
Haslam, Trudi 38
The Hatter 71, 75
Hatters, Hatters 56
Hatton, Bob 60, 90, 91, 92, 93, 95, 97, 98, 99
Hawkes, Bob 62
The Hawthorns 53, 54, 70
Heale, Gary 84, 85
Hereford United 19, 37, 42, 76
Heysel 65
Hickton, John 52
Highbury 59, 65
Hill, Ricky 10, 11, 20, 74, 75, 80, 82, 84, 86, 91, 92, 95, 97, 98
Hillsborough 17, 40
Hindson, Gordon 57
Hoddle, Glenn 74, 84, 88
Hodgson, Tom 62

23, 24, 25, 27, 28, 32, 34, 37, 38, 42, 52, 63, 72, 83
MacDougall, Ted 76
McKenzie, Duncan 50, 64
McQueen, Gordon 64
Made in Luton 30
Madeley, Paul 64
Maier, Sepp 65
Maine Road 85, 86
Manchester City 60, 67, 68, 85, 88, 90
Manchester United 17, 27, 30, 36, 54, 55, 73
the Manor Ground 52
Mansfield Town 14, 37, 85, 86, 97
Maple Road 32, 77
Maradona, Diego 10
Marsh, Rodney 20, 68, 76, 79
Match of the Day 40
Mayles, Cynthia 59
Mayles, Maurice 59
Mayles, Simon 52, 59
Messi, Lionel 27
Middlesbrough 17, 23, 28, 41, 45, 46, 49, 51, 52,
54, 58, 59, 60, 61
Midweek Football League Cup 32, 33
Mid-Week League 48, 70
Mills, David 52
Millwall 22, 24, 28, 29, 32, 41, 49, 53, 77, 79, 80,
87, 88, 94
The Mirror 44
Molineux 84
Montgomery, Jim 44
Moore, Bobby 19, 29, 30, 61, 72, 76
Moore, John 19, 37
Morecambe, Eric 10, 28, 35
The Morecambe & Wise Show 10
Moss, David 90, 91, 92, 93, 94, 95, 97, 98, 99, 100
Muller, Gerd 65

Mullery, Alan 19, 45, 72
Mum, Thelma Rance 25, 38, 42, 51, 62
Murdoch, Bobby 52
Murray, Pete 35
Newcastle Blue Star 89
Newcastle United 18, 19, 25, 37, 42, 43, 44, 60, 62, 63, 91, 93, 99
The New Forest 80
Neymar 27
Nicholl, Chris 11, 14, 18, 19, 32, 33, 34, 41, 50, 72
Northampton Town 70
Norwich City 16, 19, 73
Northern Ireland National Team 19
Nottingham Forest 20, 21, 39, 41, 42, 47, 50, 59, 71, 73, 75, 79, 82
Notts County 48, 50, 76, 80, 92, 95, 98
Nuneaton Borough 90
Oak Road End 15, 16, 19, 20, 23, 28, 29, 32, 43, 52, 64, 68, 73, 77, 80, 88, 92, 100
Oak Road Ender 93
Oak Road Enders Report 75
Oldham Athletic 83, 87, 91, 93, 95, 98
Owen, Syd 39
Oxford United 16, 38, 52, 53
Paisley, Bob 57
Parkes, Phil 45, 95
Payne, Joe 14
Pele 27
Peterborough United 90
Peters, Martin 18
Platini, Michel 65
Pleat, David 10, 87, 88, 90, 91, 93
Plymouth Argyle 14, 76, 79
Porterfield, Ian 44
Portman Road 59
Portsmouth FC 22, 29, 33, 41, 48, 71, 72

Shankly, Bill 57
Shanks, Don 29, 43, 55, 57, 59
Shanks, Wally 22
Shanks and Turner 22
Sheffield United 20, 22, 60, 63, 75, 78, 86, 87, 89, 91, 95, 96
Sheffield Wednesday 17, 24, 33, 40, 53
Shilton, Peter 20, 24, 51
Show Biz 6 35
Shrewsbury Town 14, 99
Silkman, Barry 95
Simms, Ernie 62
Simon, Sandor 70
Sissons, Johnny 24
Slough, Alan 14, 19, 24, 33, 37, 38, 72, 76
Alan Slough All Stars 72
Smith, Gary 77, 80
Sorbie, Charlie 32
Souness, Graeme 52
Southampton FC 73, 76, 80, 86, 89
The South Wales Echo 38
Spiring, Peter 60
Stamford Bridge 61, 65
Stein, Brian 10, 11, 20, 85, 86, 90, 91, 92, 93, 94, 95, 98, 99
Stephens, Kirk 11, 90, 99
Stiles, Nobby 28, 45
Stock, Alec 19, 33, 34, 37, 45
Stoke City 61, 63, 95
Suarez, Luis 27
Sunderland FC 18, 20, 22, 32, 41, 43, 44, 45, 48, 55, 73, 75, 83, 86, 93, 98
Super Furry Animals 81
Swansea City 98
Swindon Town 40, 41, 51, 90
Talbot, Brian 72, 74

Recommended relevant websites

Luton Town FC - official site
lutontown.co.uk

Hatters Heritage
hattersheritage.co.uk